John
Brown
Citrus
Publishing

**John Brown
Citrus Publishing**
The New Boathouse
136-142 Bramley Road
London W10 6SR
Tel: 020 7565 3000
info@jbcp.co.uk
www.jbcp.co.uk
Editor Andrew Losowsky
Creative director
Chris Parker
Designers Simone Carrier,
Jessica Gahan
All-time greats illustrator
James Taylor
Sub-editors Stuart
Maddison, Jeremy White
Production Carole Marz
Publisher Andy Roughton
Senior picture editor
Graham Harper
Picture editor Sally Ryall
IT manager Richard Sacre
Group creative director
Jeremy Leslie
Managing director
Dean Fitzpatrick
Chief executive
Andrew Hirsch

Colour origination
John Brown Citrus Publishing
Printer Rotolito Lombarda
Paper M-real

Published by ycn and
John Brown Citrus Publishing
© 2005

ISBN 0-9548597-1-5
978-0-9548597-1-8

ycn

Young Creatives Network
1st Floor
181 Cannon Street Road
London
E1 2LX
Tel: 020 7702 0700
info@ycnonline.com
www.ycnonline.com
Directors Nick Defty,
Dr Ben Saw

contrib

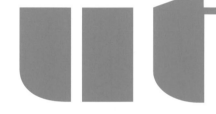

the rewards can be substantial

Welcome to book 05.06 — the third edition of our annual publication, produced once again in collaboration with John Brown Citrus Publishing.

In these pages you will find a showcase of the best work submitted as part of last year's programme, as well as this year's live creative briefs. A series of features about key industry topics, written by such figures as Adrian Shaughnessy and *Creative Review's* Patrick Burgoyne, is also inside, as is a large directory of creative agencies.

As always, this year's briefs present a diverse range of social and commercial challenges to be tackled creatively. From ending the peril of dropped chewing gum, to conceiving games for the family of 2010, these live challenges all run alongside award pools and placement schemes designed to kick start the career of anyone keen to work in the design and advertising industries.

The rewards can be substantial. On page 96, you can read the account of two ex-students who took up a placement at Saatchi & Saatchi that they received as part of their ycn award — and now they're permanent (and paid) fixtures in the agency's creative department.

Here you can see the faces of those judged to be 'best of year' as part of last year's programme. Further congratulations go to all those who also received commendations. By visiting our website, not only can you see an extended showcase of this year's commended work, plus other great submissions, but also you can learn more about ycn and our latest projects that run throughout the year.

I hope that these pages, and those online, make for inspiring reading.
Nick Defty, Director, ycn
www.ycnonline.com

The work you see showcased in this book was submitted in response to this collection of live creative briefs. The full briefs all appeared in *book 04.05,* and can be read in full at www.ycnonline.com The briefs that form the basis of this year's programme start on page 153.

last year

Britain in Europe
Produce campaign materials designed to sell the benefits of Britain's continued membership of the European Union.

Brylcreem
Build a new image for Brylcreem, using the proposition 'feel as sharp as you look' at its core.

Cabe Space
Create visual communication that will raise the profile of public parks, and inspire people to use them more.

CaféDirect
Make 5065 the preferred instant coffee brand of students.

Cancer Research UK
Motivate 18–25 year olds to take action and not burn in the sun.

Cumbria – the lake district
Develop a more contemporary appeal for Cumbria – the Lake District. It should update the image of the destination, and make it more appealing to younger age groups.

Diageo
Persuade 18–24 year olds to re-evaluate their attitudes and behaviour towards excessive (binge) drinking.

Honda
Bring the cool side of Honda to the attention of a wider audience.

Institute of Electrical Engineers
Design a piece of visual communication that will showcase the products and services of IEE.

's briefs

JBCP
Create a new magazine for people aged 60 plus.

National Geographic Channel
Produce on-air branding that will help change perceptions of the channel.

Pampers Kandoo
Increase trials of Pampers Kandoo, the first flushable toilet wipe for children.

Ribena
Make young adults proud to be seen with a Ribena Blackcurrant carton.

Skybet
Develop ambitious new ways of expressing the campaign 'It matters more when there's money on it'.

Tetra Pak
Create high awareness of the hidden benefits of cartons among secondary school children.

Virgin Mobile
Conceive a new mobile phone brand, design its visual identity and develop supporting materials.

Viz
Increase the appeal of Viz among young adults.

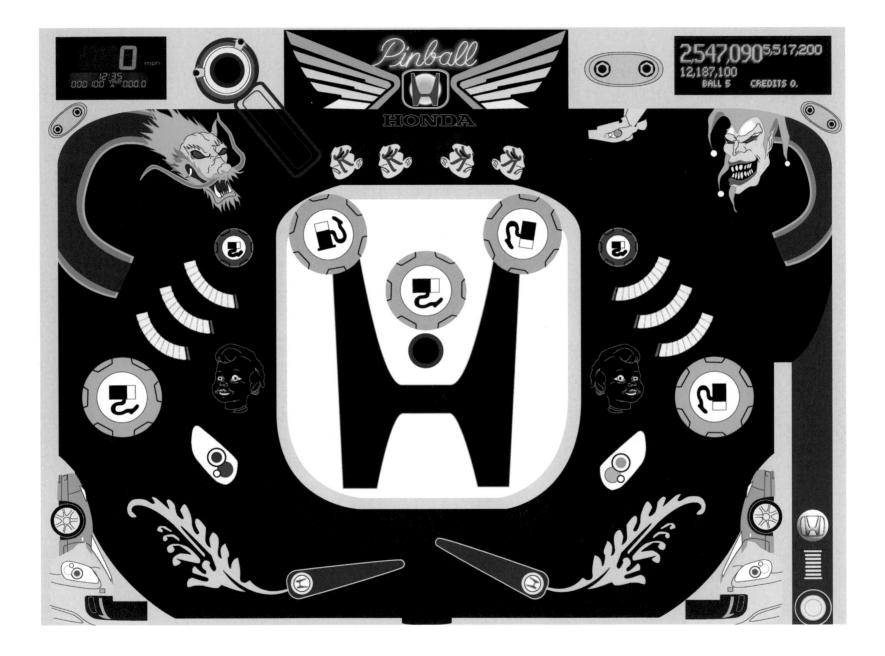

**Mark Daw &
Kooch Chung**
Commended
ycn username
DAWSVILLE2002 / KOOCH700
College Buckinghamshire
Chilterns University College
Tutors Paul Plowman, Bob
Wilkinson and Bruce Ingman

"Weird, but good weird. An idea
that held it all together.
Good technical craft, good art
direction and certainly on brief.
A load of effort, and unlike some
entries, Honda didn't feel bolted
on to a previous idea. Excellent."
**Stuart Smith – Wieden and
Kennedy**

VENUE
Anywhere in the sun, even underwater

TIMES
Find shade between 11-3 when the sun is at its hottest

DRESS
Wear a t-shirt, hat & wraparound sunglasses

COST
Your skin's health & risking your life

15+
Always use sunscreen with SPF 15 or higher

RAW

In the last 25 years the number of cases of skin cancer in 20-24 year olds has trebled. Up to 80% of cases can be prevented by reducing the amount of exposure to harmful UV rays from the sun and sunbeds.

Your chance of getting skin cancer can be drastically reduced by not getting burnt. Cover up or seek shade when the sun is at its hottest between 11-3. Wear sunscreen of SPF 15 or higher and avoid using sunbeds.

If it's caught and treated early enough it can be cured. Signs of skin cancer are moles or marks on your skin that have changed in size, shape or colour, or that itch or bleed.
For more information visit the TODAY website at www.live4today.co.uk

SunSmart Promotions
www.sunsmart.co.uk
www.live4today.co.uk
TODAY

fried

In the last 25 years the number of cases of skin cancer in 20-24 year olds has trebled. Up to 80% of cases can be prevented by reducing the amount of exposure to harmful UV rays from the sun and sunbeds.

Your chance of getting skin cancer can be drastically reduced by not getting sunburnt. Cover up or seek shade when the sun is at its hottest between 11-3. Wear sunscreen of SPF 15 or higher and avoid using sunbeds.

If it's caught and treated early enough it can be cured. Signs of skin cancer are moles or marks on your skin that have changed in size, shape or colour, or that itch or bleed.

For more information visit the TODAY website at www.live4today.co.uk

Richard Cooper
Commended

ycn username RCOOPER
College University of Derby
Tutors Leo Broadley and
Tracy Allen-Smith

"A really clever way of getting all the key messages across in an intriguing and stylish fashion, targeted directly at the youth market."

Hilary Brailey
Cancer Research UK

Steve Thone
ycn Username stevethone
College Ravensbourne College
Tutors Sian Cook, Nima
Falatoori and Finola Gaynor

Park

Something For Everyone

Winter

Spring

Summer

Autumn

Vynsie Law
Commended
ycn username VYNSIE
College Chelsea College of Art
Tutors Peter Maloney
and Tracey Waller

"Very well presented. Intelligent interpretation of park benefits, seasonality and activities. A bus stop was an excellent choice of location for display, as people will have the time and space to read it through up close."
Polly Turton – CABE Space

Anthony Burrill

Greatest comic book:
The only comic I've ever collected is *Eightball* by Dan Clowes. I love its weirdness and the strange humour. The drawing style is beautifully detailed, yet still feels fresh and alive. Parts of it are like a David Lynch film. Dark and macabre Americana, but funnier than it sounds.

Greatest clothes: Army Surplus. When I moved out of London a couple of years ago, I discovered a fantastic army surplus shop near the village where I now live. They stock incredibly practical clothing. My favourite purchase is a NATO camouflage shirt. It used to belong to somebody called OVEN, it's still got his name on the breast pocket.

Greatest celebrity: Jarvis Cocker. I always loved Pulp. I saw them play a few times and they were always great. The thing I admire about Jarvis is the way he ended Pulp and still retained his credibility.

Greatest book cover:
Somewhere Between Almost Right and Not Quite by John Baldessari. It was published to coincide with Baldessari's exhibition at the Deutsche Guggenheim, Berlin. The cover shows a black-and-white still of a tiger jumping through a hoop at a circus. The tiger has been blocked out with a flat orange silhouette, and the people in the audience have got coloured disc covering their faces. There is very simple type in the top left-hand corner, and that's it.

Greatest radio programme:
I like Radio One, but only on a Sunday morning between 5 and 7am, when my friend Chris hosts his wonderfully eclectic show. It's called *The Blue Room*, and he plays suitably early morning post-club music, mainly down-tempo electronica.
Anthony Burrill is a graphic designer.
www.anthonyburrill.com

Public Parks
for peace of mind

Parks and other public spaces are for everyone, places to live and breathe, walk and run, rest or play. They are where we meet together, where we stop to reflect, where we revive our spirits.

Jonathan Clements
Commended

ycn username CASIMER1

College University College, Falmouth

Tutors Sue Miller, Mark Woodhams and John Unwin

"Simple and clever thinking that goes beyond a simple health message. Parks and human beings are seen as natural systems. Independent of space, but suggests green space through use of tree motif and colour. This could apply to anyone, anywhere. Supporting sketch book demonstrated an excellent thought process and consideration of issues."

Polly Turton – CABE Space

cabe space
www.cabespace.org

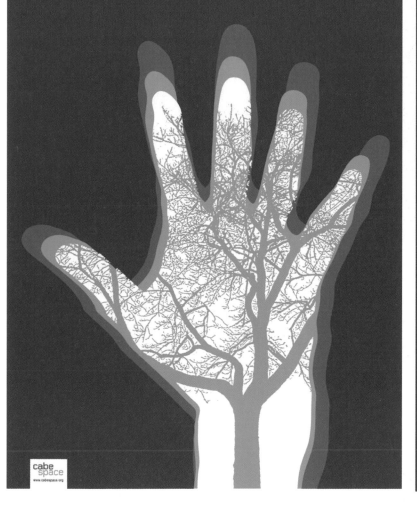

Public Parks

nature first-hand

Parks and other public spaces are for everyone, places to live and breathe, walk and run, rest or play. They are where we meet together, where we stop to reflect, where we revive our spirits.

cabe
space
www.cabespace.org

Public Parks

a breath of fresh air

Parks and other public spaces are for everyone, places to live and breathe, walk and run, rest or play. They are where we meet together, where we stop to reflect, where we revive our spirits.

cabe
space
www.cabespace.org

Graeme Hastings
Commended
ycn username
GRAEMEHASTINGS
"We loved the tongue-in-cheek humour behind this one. The copy was really well written – informative and humorous, not an easy combination to get right."
Hilary Brailey
Cancer Research UK

Pete Cutler
ycn username rev

12 months in design

BY PATRICK BURGOYNE

Offshoring

Will design be the next industry to see jobs disappearing offshore? Where the IT and customer service industries have gone before, design and the creative industries may be about to follow. US outsourcing specialist Office Tiger has established an operation in Chennai, India specifically to cater for design work. It's been busily buying up scarce design talent across the subcontinent, offering wages way above local competitors. Those wages, however, are still between a twentieth and a tenth of what a designer would be paid in the UK. Now that procurement managers are bringing their calculators to bear on advertising and design work – buying the latter with the same cold, numerical logic with which they purchase paperclips – the huge potential cost savings may prove impossible for clients to ignore. It won't be the high-end, conceptual projects that are at risk but the grunt work – the implementation of huge corporate identities, the repurposing of ads to different formats, the production of lengthy business documents and presentations. Not pretty, but good for the cash flow, particularly for the bigger branding groups. We've got used to the idea of our trainers and our technology being made in the developing world, so why not the materials used to promote them?

Plush

Vinyl toys? So last year. The future of designer desk decoration is knitted. Plush or plushies are the next wave in creative collectibles. The craze started, inevitably, in Japan. The Japanese love of

characterisation, plus the growing desire for hand-made, customised products in the face of mass consumer goods, kicked off a craze for all manner of curious, cuddly critters. The US has embraced the movement in a big way with a travelling exhibition, Plushastrophe, carrying plushes from more than 40 different makers, including Friends With You, Uglydolls and Shawnimals. Nearly all the makers are graphic designers, illustrators or artists. Many plushes are one-offs, standing in marked contrast to the moulded slickness of vinyl toys. Plushes are made to be played with, not placed reverentially on a shelf. Unlike their vinyl cousins, they seldom come in fancy packaging, and revel in being slightly frayed around the edges. They want to be loved, not worshipped.

Magazine distribution

This may sound boring, but stick with me. In Britain right now, it is possible to walk into any newsagent on any high street, and choose from a huge variety of magazines. Whatever your interest, from *Angling Times* to *Zoo*, you can find something. That may be about to change. The Office of Fair Trading is looking into the way in which magazines are distributed in the UK. Currently, one distributor holds a monopoly in each region of the country. As a result, even small, remote newsagents usually carry a wide array of titles. The OFT thinks this is anti-competitive. It's right, it is. But the consequences of breaking up the system could be disastrous for the British magazine industry. In the US, when a similar situation was resolved by opening up distribution to the market, 32,000 newsagents were forced

to close. In turn, many magazines disappeared as well. And it wasn't the big boys. If something similar happens in the UK, the titles in danger will be the specialist titles. The small, interesting magazines, not the huge money-making machines. It's a good time for independent magazines right now – there are more than ever before, many with strong, innovative designs. If these disappear, the newsstand will be a very bland place indeed.

What is design?

We all enjoy a good row, especially one involving the great and good. But the drama at the Design Museum last October, while undoubtedly fun to observe from a distance, also touched on a fundamental debate in the industry. What do we mean by design? James Dyson resigned from the chair of the Design Museum in protest at what he saw as a shift away from the institution's principals toward froth and frippery. The Museum, he huffed, was not set up to celebrate flower arranging. In Dyson's view, design is about engineering, invention and the manufacturing process, not style or communication. Design Museum director Alice Rawsthorn, however, had been attempting to widen the Museum's portfolio to pay more attention to graphics, to fashion and to new media. She recognises that design is also about communication, and her policy has proved immensely successful with visitors, numbers having risen 20 per cent. After such a high-profile ding-dong, you may have thought that Rawsthorn would have been content to stay out of the limelight for a little while, but further controversy followed with the award of the

Museum's Designer of the Year prize to the Design Council Director, Hilary Cottam, who, while being hugely talented at many things, is not a designer. What she does do, however, is facilitate design, and make the case for the design process to be applied in unexpected areas, to find solutions for all manner of problems. Cottam believes that design can make our lives better in all kinds of ways. Who could argue with that?

Grrr

Most ad agency client presentations involve polyboard, lots of slick chat and some very overpriced tea and biscuits. To demonstrate their idea for a new Honda commercial, Wieden + Kennedy creatives Richard Russell, Sean Thompson and Michael Russoff decided to sing. Their little ditty was all about hate. The idea: that hate can be a positive thing if it induces one to change something for the better – in this case, a diesel engine. Honda's chief engineer, so the story goes, hated diesel engines with a passion, vowing never to sully one of his cars with such an abomination unless he could design one himself from scratch. This he did, producing, Honda claims, a far quieter, cleaner engine. After hearing the team's song, an appropriately gobsmacked Honda client Simon Thompson decreed that not one note must change. Directors Smith & Foulkes threw the kitchen sink at the commercial, producing a riot of candy coloured kitsch. Wieden + Kennedy persuaded Garrison Keillor to record the soundtrack over the telephone, accompanied by the creative team themselves, and the awards rolled in. I was on a jury for the pan–European

Epica awards in November. Usually, the process of deciding on the Grand Prix is a lengthy, passionate affair, amply demonstrating the ability of the various peoples of Europe to come together and get on each other's tits. This time though, we were finished in five minutes. After one vote and no debate, Grrr was the runaway winner. Voting over and time for some Slovenian wine. A similar pattern unfolded at the rest of the year's awards shows as Grrr swept all before it, including two gold D&AD pencils. And to think that car ads used to be riddled with boring clichés.

Communicate

Here's a brief: sum up 40 years of British graphic design in one, smallish, exhibition. An impossible ask, but impossible to refuse. For the Barbican's 'Communicate' show, design critic and curator Rick Poynor chose to focus on what he termed "independent" graphic design. This term, he said, applied to designers who have kept their studios small, who retain the freedom to choose their clients and collaborators, and whose priority is to create work of the highest quality. He drew a parallel with independent filmmakers and record labels to illustrate this idea. Of course, the resultant show was personal and featured only a selection of design work produced since the 60s; how could it be otherwise? But designer Quentin Newark was far from happy. In an explosive exchange of views in *Creative Review,* Newark accused Poynor of using his "independent" tag to "mask personal prejudice" in selecting the show's content. "A lot of the designers who

ClearviewHwy-5-W

feature prominently in the show are people you are familiar with, even friends with, and a lot of those you have omitted you either haven't met, or are seen by you as somehow reactionary or jaded," he argued. Newark also questioned Poynor's criteria for selecting the work, the show's lack of explanatory text, and its authority. But the public loved it, with the Barbican far exceeding its estimates for visitor numbers. Incomplete it may have been, but how often does graphic design enjoy such public recognition?

Typography saves lives

Graphic designers yearn to be taken seriously, to feel as if they are making a contribution to the betterment of the world rather than contributing to rampant consumerism. Every so often, a project comes along that makes the whole industry feel a little better about itself. Fourteen years ago, signage designer Donald Meeker thought he could make a difference. An ageing US driver population presented highway authorities with a problem. Older drivers took longer to make decisions. They found roadsigns more difficult to read than their younger peers, in part because of "halation" where, in bright light, a halo effect forms around lettering. Reduced decision-making ability means reduced braking times and increased accident rates. In addition, US authorities were attempting to load more and more information onto their signage systems, to cope with new instructional regimes and additional tourist information. The answer, so the authorities thought, was to increase the overall size of the signs themselves, an operation that could cost millions. Meek thought that, through better

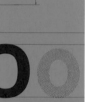

1:5.1 stroke width-to-he

100.0 mm

75.0 mm

nway Gothic Series E
wy-5-W

typography, signs could be made more legible and fit more information without increasing the overall size. With the help of type designer James Montalbano, he created a new typeface, Clearview, which dramatically improved legibility and, thus, increased stopping distances, helping to avoid accidents and, ultimately, save lives.
In September 2004, Clearview was approved by the US highway authorities. All this was achieved with virtually no funding. Meeker and Montalbano believed in what they were doing and kept at it. They showed that designers could solve a problem that previously had been left up to engineers. Good typography saves lives.

The new wave

Over the past year, there has been something of a generational shift in the UK graphic design scene. Until now, we thought of studios such as North, Tom Hingston Studio, Browns and The Designers Republic as the bright young things of the industry. But North is ten years old this year, and TDR have been going for an incredible 19. Designers who learned their trade in such studios have now reached the point where they are itching to break out on their own. A rush of start-ups has established a new wave of UK graphics studios. Studio Thomson (ex-Yacht Associates and Aboud Sodano), Universal Everything (ex-TDR), YES Studio (ex-Blue Source), Bibliotheque (ex-Farrow and North), Tappin Gofton (ex-Hingston and Blue Source respectively) and Tiller Williams (ex-David James and Martin Jacobs) have all formed in the past year. And the most talked-about graphic designer of the year was ex-TDR Michael C Place. It's an exciting time for the

UK graphics scene, although it must be an awkward development for the founders of the studios these young bloods have left behind. How do you cope with design middle age?

Honourable mentions

• Channel Four on-air identity: the only rival to Honda Grrr in the awards stakes this year. A beautifully realised, witty identity campaign, bringing Martin Lambie-Nairn's self-assembling figure four into the twenty-first century.
• *Great Ideas – 20 fabulous book covers*: a testament to the power of typography to convey complex ideas and emotions.
• Impossible Sprint: TBWA\Japan staged a 50-metre sprint up the side of a Hong Kong skyscraper for adidas. In advertising, commercials are no longer enough.
• Soulwax: Trevor Jackson's Op Art proves that there's still life in record-sleeve design.

Patrick Burgoyne is editor of Creative Review

DESIGNER- MARTIN SHARP. OZ NO.7, MAGAZINE COVER, NOVEMBER 1967.
DESIGNER- SCOTT KING, SLEAZENATION VOL.4 NO.1 MAGAZINE COVER WITH "CHER GUEVARA" IMAGE BY KING, FEBRUARY 2001.
DESIGNER- DAVID KING, "STOP THE NATIONAL FRONT" POSTER FOR ANTI-NAZI LEAGUE, 1978 ©DAVID KING COLLECTION.
DESIGNER- ROBERT BROWNJOHN. 'OBSESSION AND FANTASY' . POSTER FOR ROBERT FRASER GALLERY, LONDON, 1957. PHOTOGRAPH ©DAVID KING COLLECTION

Ella Howell
ycn Username ella
College Loughborough
University
Tutor Anne Brookes

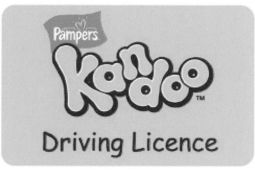

Jeniffer Bostock
Commended
ycn username BOOZE_MONKEY
College De Montfort University
Tutors Ian Newsham, John Crawford, Alec Robertson and Emma Powell

"Always great to see ideas that will help kids keep themselves engaged and entertained during a shopping trip with mum or dad."
George Eapen – Pampers

Chris Coulson &
Amy Hornett
Commended
ycn username CWISS
College Buckinghamshire Chilterns University College
Tutors Paul Plowman, Bob Wilkinson, Bruce Ingman and Julie Wright

"Creative concept that is fun, exciting, and empowering to kids. Also adds excitement to kids' toilet decor in supermarkets (could also extend to theme parks nurseries etc.)"
George Eapen – Pampers

Where Do You Park For Fun?

WE PROVIDE A PLACE FOR FUN, GAMES AND NATURE
MORE INFORMATION AT YOUR LOCAL TOURIST INFORMATION + WWW.CABESPACE.ORG.UK

cabe space

Where Do You Park For Life?

WE PROVIDE A PLACE FOR LIFE, PEACE AND REFLECTION
MORE INFORMATION AT YOUR LOCAL TOURIST INFORMATION + WWW.CABESPACE.ORG.UK

cabe space

Lars Højberg
Commended
ycn username THESELFIMAGES
College University College
Falmouth
Tutors John Unwin and
Sue Miller

"Very professional presentation.
Good use of visuals and play on
the word 'park'. Evocative of
seasonality of parks, especially
hazy urban summers and
festivals in parks."
Polly Turton – CABE Space

Matthew Lewis

Greatest TV Series:
I am Alan Partridge. British sitcom at its best. Every episode full of classic, cringe-worthy moments.

Greatest photographer:
Any elderly relatives of mine could qualify, for simple reasons: the often-accidental compositions produce unexpected delights that prove that a trained eye doesn't always produce the best images. There are also the colours, beautiful sepia tones.

Greatest album:
Kid A by Radiohead for me is sublimely restless mood music. Elusive and aloof.

Greatest videogame:
Never really been into video games, but hard to dispute the addictiveness that is Tetris. Problem solving at its purest!

Greatest quotation:
'Uh, gee, great.' Andy Warhol.
Matthew's work is on page 110.

Jamie Boyd
Commended
ycn username JAMWIDGE
College University College
Falmouth
Tutors John Unwin
and Mark Woodhams
"A brilliantly conceived and very
well-thought-through brand

name. This work was very well
executed and excellent attention
has been given to detail.
The demonstrated packaging
presents the product well and
the supporting advertising was,
importantly, very believable."
Damian Schnabel
– Virgin Mobile

Gareth Ball
Commended
ycn username GARETHB_21
College Hull College
Tutors Isabel Willock and
Chris Dimmack
"Irreverent and very engaging.
This idea was perfectly adapted
for web too."
Hilary Brailey
Cancer Research UK

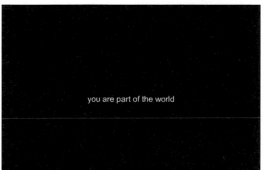

you are part of the world

think again

Norie Honda
Commended
ycn username NORIE
College Northbrook College
Tutor Priscilla Macintosh
"We loved this. A guy watching the TV with the world unfolding behind him really works."
Justin O'Sullivan – National Geographic Channel

Mutiat Gbadamosi
Commended

ycn username MORENIKE

"This was really in line with the Kandoo empowerment equity, and in a kid-friendly design that could be nicely linked with health professionals."

George Eapen – Pampers

1. Shrink wrapped trial pack
2. Trial pack slip case
3. Information booklet for mums
4. Kandoo carry wallet
5. Pocket sample wipes

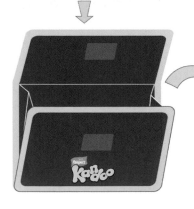

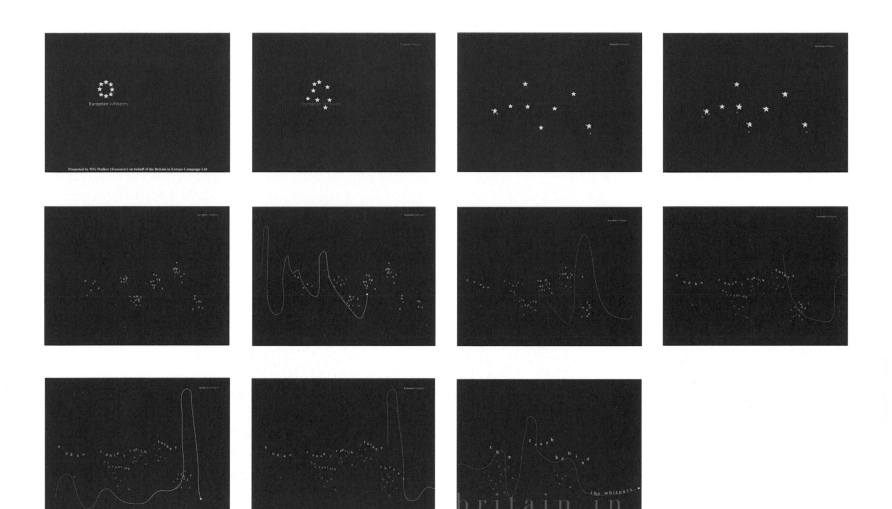

Gail Plackett
Commended
ycn username GPLACKETT
College University College
Northampton
Tutor Barry Wenden

"A really engaging and creative take on a far-from-simple subject matter."

Lucy Powell
Britain in Europe

Rodney Boot
Commended
ycn username BOOTRJ
College University College
Falmouth
Tutors Mark Woodhams
and Jon Unwin

"One of the few ad campaigns
to have a clear line of attack.
Relevant choice of illustration
and colour. Some strong,
simple copy."
Neil McLeod – Café Direct

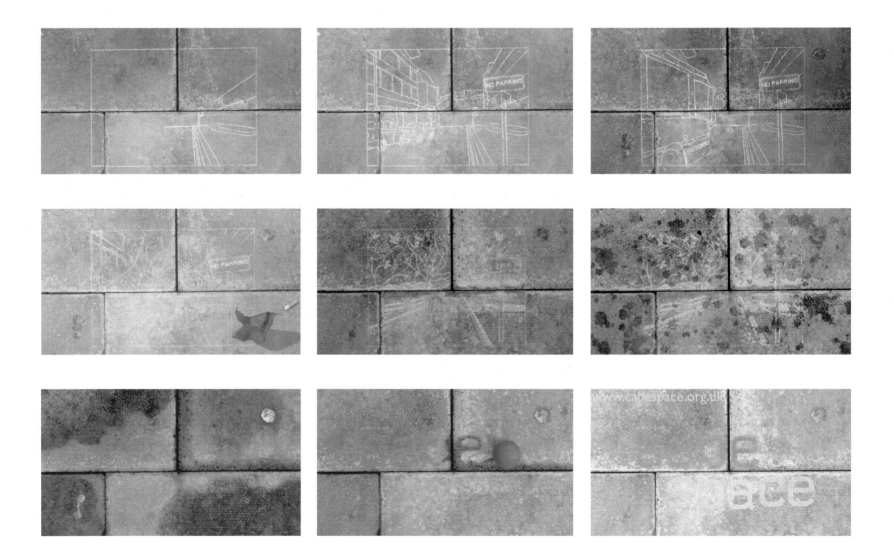

**Liz Bennett &
Jen Clayton**
ycn username J_CLAY82
College Leeds
Metropolitan University
Tutors Andy Edwards and
Mick Marsden

Martin Taylor
Commended
ycn username SMELLYCAT
College Bath Spa
University College
Tutor Tim Vyner
and Neil Jenkins

"A very subtle concept that
works really well."
**Justin O'Sullivan –
National Geographic Channel**

1. Living room scene, cat asleep on sofa.

Sound: Gentle breathing from cat.

2. View closes in on the cat sleeping.

Sound: Gentle breathing from cat.

3. Cat wakes up and looks at viewer.

Sound: Subtle 'purr' noise

4. Cat begins to yawn and strange spots begin to appear
over it's face and body.
Sound: Cat yawning.

5. Cat briefly morphs into a leopard, also yawning.

Sound: Cat/leopard yawning.

6. Cat turns back to normal as it finishes yawning.

Sound: Subtle cat 'purr'.

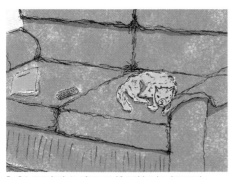

7. Cat goes back to sleep as if nothing has happened.

Sound: Gentle breathing from cat.

Think Again...

8. Fades to the National Geographic tag line.

Sound: Gentle breathing from cat.

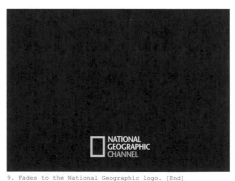

NATIONAL
GEOGRAPHIC
CHANNEL

9. Fades to the National Geographic logo. [End]

Sound: Gentle breathing from cat.

BIG BROTHER

Izabella Bielawska

Greatest book:
Amusing Ourselves to Death by Neil Postman. It combines two science-fiction novels – Orwell's *1984* and Huxley's *Brave New World*.

Greatest website:
Guardian Unlimited (www.guardian.co.uk). It's great for project research.

Greatest phrase:
"Graphic design is a language, not a message", said by Tibor Kalman. Simple and very true.

Greatest photograph:
Any photograph by David LaChappelle. He creates a beautifully surreal story in every image. There are so many details to discover.

Greatest brand:
Benrik Ltd. Better than Apple, more refreshing than Coke... and they make me laugh.

Izabella Bielawska is a recent design graduate who produced the exhibition graphics for this year's ycn second round of judging.

VIZ

'Brown Bear's nose'

n. a cute little round turd that hibernates at the bottom of the pan.

Taken from Roger's Profanasaurus
www.viz.co.uk

VIZ

'Doggies'

n. Intercourse in the position adopted by dogs, usually near some dustbins

Taken from Roger's Profanasaurus
www.viz.co.uk

VIZ

'Mr Whippy's in town'

euph. Declaration that all is not well in the chamber of horrors.

Taken from Roger's Profanasaurus
www.viz.co.uk

VIZ

'Mumra'

n. The act of sneaking behind your mother and shouting RAAAAR.

Taken from Roger's Profanasaurus
www.viz.co.uk

Sally Turbutt
Commended
ycn username SWEEBY
College University of Lincoln
Tutors Julie Husband
and Alex Raybone
"A nice, simple and effective response to the brief. Great idea for a *Viz* ad campaign as the visual treatment ads to the text-only nature of the *Profanisaurus*."
Will Watt – Viz comic

Tom Poland
ycn username thuglife
College University College
Falmouth
Tutor John Unwin

BRYLCREEM

LOYALTY IS EARNED, TRADITION IS KEPT, AND STYLE IS A WAY OF LIFE.

mohican   razor   flip   urban   kick   sweep

"THIS IS ONE **PRODUCT NOT** TO BE **MISSED**, ALL PERFORMANCES ARE AS **SHARP** AS THEY **LOOK**. THE BEST **BRITISH** PRODUCT I HAVE **USED** IN YEARS."

Lee Chapman
Commended
ycn username LEE_C
College University of
Gloucestershire
Tutors Vicky Baker and
Mike Abbey

"An excellent interpretation of
the brief, producing a strong
idea that provides the
opportunity to showcase the
entire range. Beautifully
presented."
Sam Cooper – Brylcreem

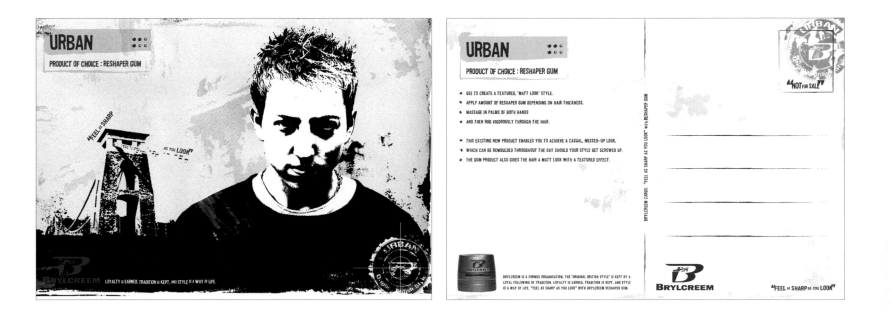

Collector Cards

Each card has its collectors number

The backs of each card, a picture of the product is shown and a description is given of how each product works.

These collectors card will be available on shop counters where the product is sold and in fashionable clothes shops.

The faces are cut out, which enables you to place the card over your passport photograph, replacing your hair style with the style on the card, so you can see how the hair style looks on yourself. Or you can look through the hole at someone elses face.

Kevin Grennan
ycn username kevgrenn
College Limerick Institute of Technology

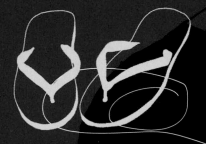

thomas.matthews

Greatest illustrator:
Andy Smith. We love him.
www.asmithillustration.com

Greatest product:
Grande café latte.

Greatest joke:
What do you call a French
man wearing sandals?
Phillipe Phillop.

Greatest galleries: Whitney
Gallery, New York; Tate Modern;
Pitt Rivers (though it's more
of a museum).

Greatest flag:
Skull and crossbones.
thomas.matthews agency was
founded by Sophie Thomas and
Kristine Matthews in 1997.
www.thomasmatthews.com

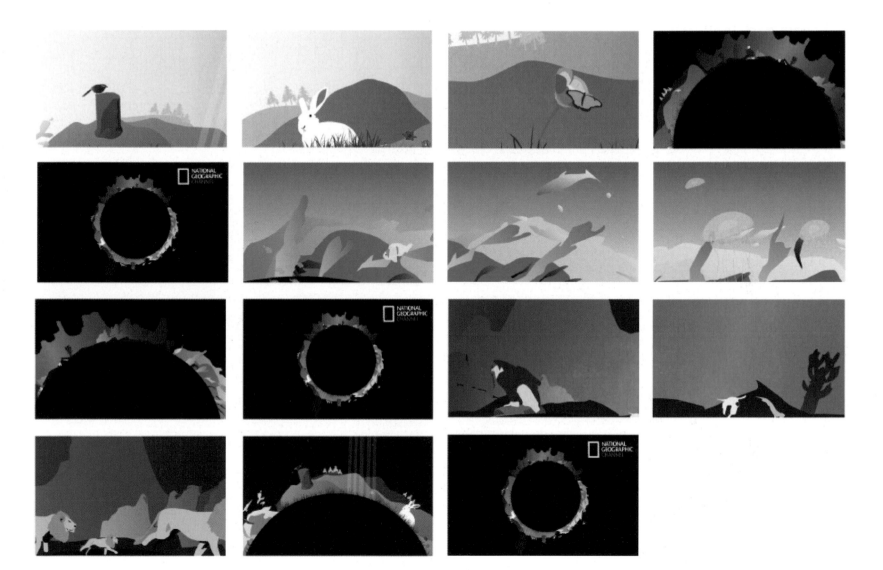

Craig Lewisohn
ycn username bing3000
College Nottingham Trent University
Tutors Robert Newton and Robert Harland

Lise Marie Hoffmeyer
Commended
ycn username LISE
College Ravensbourne College
Tutor Liz Friedman
"Great use of space on and in public transport. Green footsteps might add to street clutter, but a lovely concept. Demonstrates an excellent overall understanding of green space issues, and the design, layout and use of the urban environment."
Polly Turton – CABE Space

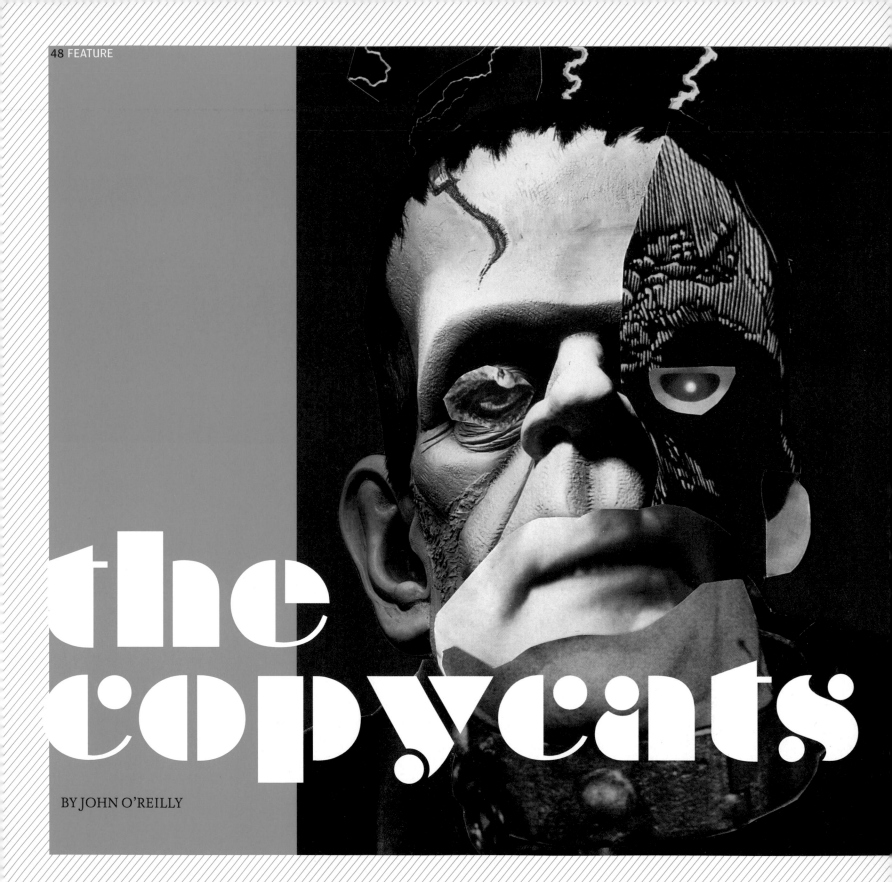

the copycats

BY JOHN O'REILLY

Original doesn't exist. The original, the completely new is an ideal, a myth, a paradox. If something were unique or original as to be nothing like anything that has ever gone before, we would probably not be able to recognise or understand it. The truth is that what we call 'original work' is always built from the familiar and the known.

In advertising and design, as with all creative industries, originality is about reworking and reframing ideas, materials, imagery and words. Sometimes, the influence is obvious, part of the creation even: Steve McQueen's character Bullitt is reframed in a Ford Puma ad; Gene Kelly in *Singing in the Rain* becomes a break dancer for Volkswagen.

How – or if – you should credit your influences is not just a creative question. Increasingly, it's a legal question as well. When do reference and allusion become a matter for the lawyers? Is one person's homage another person's plagiarism?

Original horror
Michele Jannuzzi, Director of Jannuzzi Smith Design, argues that originality is different to creativity. "If I think of all the ideas I had in my career, I would like to think I had one original idea. Between the colour period and the two versions of cubism, even Picasso maybe had three in his life, quite prolific – or maybe one original idea that was camouflaged into three or even two."

Jannuzzi was once asked to create a stamp for the Royal Mail. It was a first-day cover for a set of stamps titled 'Tales of Terror' (Dracula, Frankenstein, Dr Jekyll and Mr Hyde, The Hound of Baskervilles).

"We wanted to make a Frankenstein out of all other Frankensteins. None of the images we were using was original. Not even the thought of making Frankenstein out of different bodies was original. That is the *Frankenstein* story itself!"

He didn't invent photomosiacs, yet Jannuzzi's concept still felt original because it involved taking an aspect from the original story and using the technique to make this aspect literal in the image. "We were playing with a character that had had a lot of interpretations throughout history in illustration, painting, movies – and we would create a new Frankenstein made up of other Frankensteins. Nothing we were using was original, but the idea we were adding on was original."

Originality and the divine spark
Jannuzzi's work captures the creative, philosophical and legal dimensions of originality. Mary Shelley's 19th-century story *Frankenstein* gave fictional birth to the emerging ideas of 'genius' and 'originality'. Immanuel Kant once wrote: "Genius sets its own rules. Genius is totally contrary to the spirit of imitation."

Frankenstein is the ultimate expression of human creativity and imagination – a power previously held by God, imagination itself this time providing the divine spark. For art directors and designers, this desire for originality defines the task in hand. Create don't imitate.

Originality is usually a client's stated desire, for very different reasons. No matter how similar they are to their rivals, companies trade on the idea of originality. In business speak, originality is the Unique Selling Point.

But go too far with originality in communication, and the user base can get confused. You need a very strong brand indeed in order to risk taking your customers somewhere they haven't previously associated with your industry. And of course, if you succeed, your rivals won't be far behind.

Originality and threats
On 23 June this year, music news website pitchforkmedia.com published a story about Nike's promotion for their 'Major Threat' 2005 American east-coast tour. The publicity material showed a blue-tinted image of a man sitting on some steps, head folded in his arms, with the words 'Major Threat' running down the side.

Alongside this image, pitchfork ran an image of a man sitting on some steps, head folded in his arms, with the words 'Minor Threat' running down the side. It was the cover art for band Minor Threat's 1984 compilation album. They quoted a spokesman from Minor Threat's label, complaining that Nike had stolen the image, immorally trying to link the ethos of the band's alternative skate culture with their brand.

There was no doubting the inspiration – indeed, the tour might have been named principally with the visual image in mind. The label hinted at potential lawsuits. Four days later, Nike ran a full apology, promising to dispose of all flyers and publicity material containing the image, saying: "Nike Skateboarding's 'Major Threat' tour poster was designed, executed and promoted by skateboarders, for skateboarders. All of Nike employees responsible for the creation of the tour flyer are fans of both Minor Threat and

BY JANNUZZI SMITH FOR "TALES OF TERROR" STAMPS PACK, ROYAL MAIL, 1997.
1&3 FRANKENSTEIN OR THE MODERN PROMETHEUS, MARY WOLLSTONECRAFT SHELLEY, ILLUSTRATED BY BARRY MOSER, UNIVERSITY OF CALIFORNIA PRESS, 1984
2 FRANKENSTEIN, BLUCK & LAW, 1996
4 FRANKENSTEIN AND THE MONSTER FROM HELL, HAMMER FILMS, 1973
5&7 BIG FRANK, HASBRO INTERNATIONAL INC., 1995
6 FRANKENSTEIN, THAMES TELEVISION, 1968
8 THE HORROR OF FRANKENSTEIN, HAMMER FILMS, 1968

EMPICS

Dischord Records, and have nothing but respect for both. Minor Threat's music and iconographic album cover have been an inspiration to countless skateboarders since the album came out in 1984. And for members of the Nike Skateboarding staff, this is no different. This was a poor judgement call and should not have been executed without consulting Minor Threat and Dischord Records."

Nike is a brand renowned for its streetwise advertising and marketing, in the past using renowned off-mainstream directors from Spike Lee to Spike Jonze. In this instance, they attempted an open homage, as so many have done in the past. It's a potentially great piece of communication, flattering its audience with its reference to an obscure 1980s punk band. But it backfired and the backlash was considered too damaging to continue with the image.

Legally, Nike may have been safe, as they were creating a clear homage to the original piece. The larger problem was around the attempt to appropriate a punk band's anarchism for their own commercial intentions – and so they were accused of plagiarism. It was the potential for bad publicity that led them swiftly to withdraw.

Where does homage and influence begin, and where does it fall into plagiarism? After all, Minor Threat's own album artwork was heavily influenced by trends in early 1980s design. Perhaps it's not about original work at all, but the concept and intentions behind it. Legally, intention is notoriously hard to prove, but the audience will make up its own mind very quickly, as Nike surmised.

Originality and moustaches

Another controversial set of ads was the WCRS campaign for directory enquiry number 118 118. The campaign swamped all other brands in this new market. Creative Director Tim Robertson explains, "It's one of those campaigns that divides people, like the best campaigns sometimes do. It's easy to not like it, but it's very difficult to not remember it. The whole point in this new deregulated industry was to establish the number as firmly as possible, and so a given for us was getting 118 118 under people's skin."

It got up the nose of one individual in particular. The moustachioed identical twin runners became the subject of a complaint to regulatory board Ofcom by athlete David Bedford, who insisted the ads were using his image. Ofcom didn't ask for the ad campaign's withdrawal, but it did uphold that this *was* a caricature of the runner. However, Ofcom also denied that people watching the ad would believe Bedford had endorsed it. What the campaign conveyed was a certain kind of obsession, and made people forget about the probable grim reality of the call centre.

In many respects, you could argue that the ruling was creatively odd. What does caricature mean when you are supposedly caricaturing an 'original' that in all honestly few people know? For most viewers of the ad, who weren't experts in 1970s athletics, the experience of the 118 118 'David Bedford' caricature would have preceded their experience of 'the original' David Bedford.

And why would you nail your new product specifically to a relatively obscure figure from

the 1970s? From a creative point of view, the only way in which using such an obscure figure as 'caricature' would make sense is if the whole thing had been engineered from the very beginning as a PR stunt.

Originality and ideas

Some say that the only way to protect your idea from plagiarism or unwanted homage is to try to do something so specific that it cannot be copied. In an interview for ad industry bible *Lurzer's Archive*, Ron Seichrist, one of the founders of the Miami Ad School along with his wife Pippa, argues that, "You can't protect an idea, you know, it's out there, belongs to anybody, so don't worry about it. Just do something that someone else can't do with it."

There again, sometimes designers are desperate not to appear original. When trying to persuade a difficult client about some ground-breaking work that you really believe in, the best approach is often to suggest that it was really the client's idea in the first place.

John O'Reilly is a design writer and editor of Edit *for Getty Images*

The untouchables

When is a colour not a colour? When it's the subject of a legal battle. Orange mobile phones took the easyGroup to court when the Easy brand moved into mobile phones. Orange had registered Pantone colour No.151 for phones and phone services, but lawyers question whether this protects them against other companies using different shades of orange. The easyGroup equally relies on orange for its general branding – in its case, No.021. At the time of writing, the case has still not been resolved.

Yellow pantone No.109 has been registered by the AA as their colour in the area of recovery vehicles, while BP registered green pantone No.348c as a significant element of its brand identity, and won the court case against a rival petrol company that created the industry precedent on colour ownership.

It's not just logos or colours that are often copyright protected. When it was launching in China, Crayola trademarked the smell of its crayons, and Rolls-Royce did the same for the smell of the interior of its cars. Peugeot went one further – when referring to cars, all three-digit numbers with a zero in the middle officially belong to them.

PANTONE®
151 U

PANTONE®
Orange 021 U

PANTONE®
109 U

PANTONE®
348 U

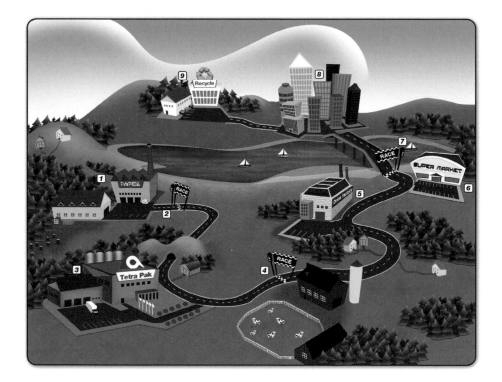

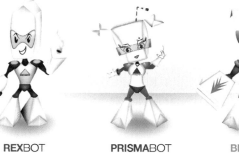

REXBOT   PRISMABOT   BRICKBOT

Olof Jönnerstig
Commended
ycn username FLOWECHO
College University of Lincoln
Tutor James O'Leary

"The innovative use of computer-based communication engages the target market in a medium that they are highly receptive to. Olof has not only created a story through which teenagers can learn about the benefits of cartons, but also encourages them to learn with appealing, retro characters, as they try to win the game. Well done Olof!"

Jon Rose – Tetra Pak

Ruth Claw
Commended
ycn username TYLER
College Hastings College
Tutor David Fowler

"A creative concept that is empowering, fun, exciting, and adaptable for young boys and girls alike. Could also extend to be a Kandoo personal hygiene bag."
George Eapen – Pampers

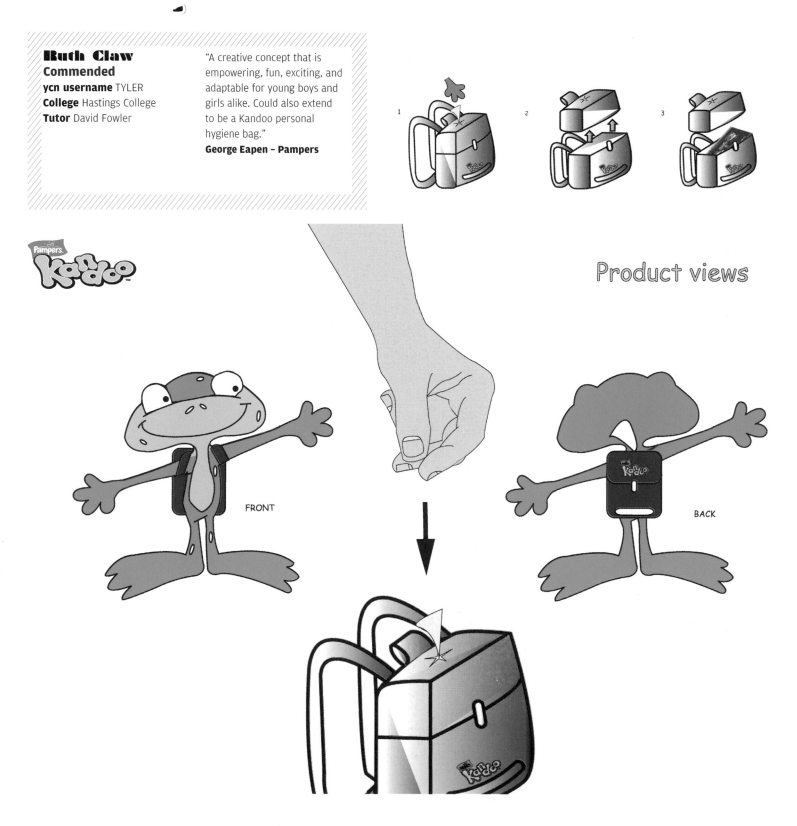

Product views

FRONT

BACK

It matters more when there's money on it   skybet

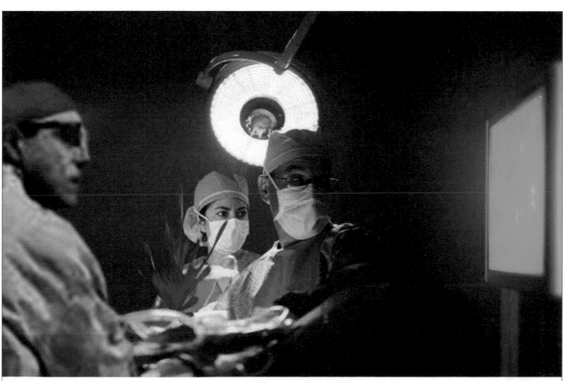

It matters more when there's money on it   skybet

Russell Borger & Elwin Vizetelly de Groot

ycn username ELWIN11

"Distinctive, original, funny and on brief. This campaign communicated the thought of "it matters more when there's money on it" via the idea that the experience of having a bet on distracts you from your immediate surroundings. More generally, what interested us was Russell and Elwins' bravery in not featuring any sport whatsoever. Other campaigns had inched away from showing sport without freeing themselves entirely. It is a unique and ambitious bookmaker who bucks the trend and promotes betting on an emotional benefit, rather than referring to what you can bet on. It's bang on strategy for a brand like Skybet."

Ed Collin - Mother

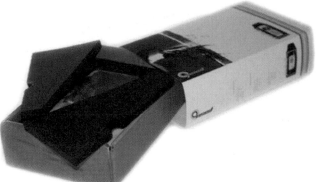

**Ryan Dilley &
Ross Stirling**
Commended
ycn username RYANDILLEY /
NAUGHTY
College University of
Gloucestershire
Tutors Vicky Baker and
Paul Wilson

"The packaging was certainly
different, achieving real stand
out with a great urban and
youth-orientated look and feel.
The inclusion of user guides and
POS solutions made this a first-
class and comprehensive piece
of work."
Damian Schnabel – Virgin Mobile

Banisha Masuria
Commended
ycn username MASURIA
College Dunstable College
Tutors Malcolm Jobling
and Celeste Henney

"This campaign is clearly more adult than we have ever been on Ribena. In that respect, it does the job in terms of updating the brand for adults, although I don't think we would ever go down such a sexually explicit route on this brand."
Chris Trapps – Ribena

Helen Murgatroyd

Greatest advert: The Tropicana press ads, with the cartons made to look like oranges in a string bag, are fantastic. I love the eyecatching imagery with the clever yet simple concept behind it.

Greatest car: The original Mini Cooper. It's got novelty super-safe windows for rear passengers, and a suprisingly roomy boot for bric-a-brac.

Greatest painting: Diagonal by Euan Uglow. The spacious composition is dramatic. I really like the black marks left from Uglow's complex measuring system – they give the painting an element of a raw 'work in progress', and leave no pretence.

Greastest cartoon character: Danger Mouse's sidekick, Ernest Penfold. Those black-rimmed glasses make him irresistable.

Greatest website: The intro to www.scandinaviandesign.com has a fun, minimal design. If you roll your mouse over the red telephone-style object, it will turn into 40 chairs, and other miscellaneous pieces of household furniture. It's a playful bit of design. Though I didn't get much further than that page.

Helen's work is on page 86

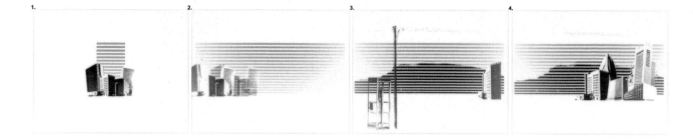

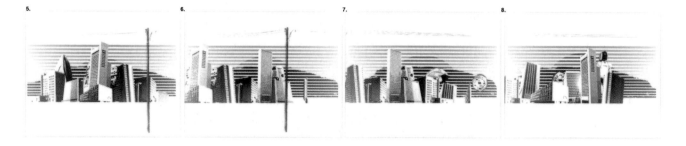

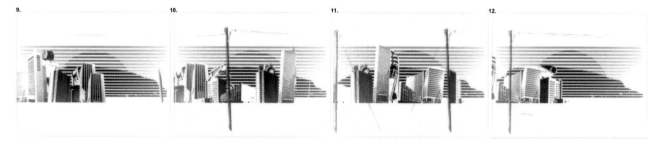

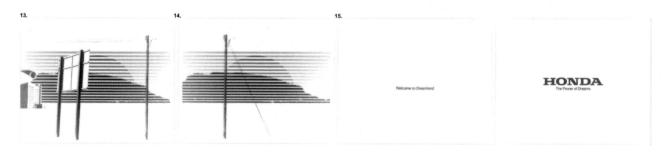

Mark Thompson
ycn username Thunderwing
College University College
Falmouth
Tutor Mafalda Spencer

Steven Clarkson
Commended
ycn username CLARKS05
College Liverpool John Moores
Tutors Carole Potter, Seel
Garside and Ian Mitchell
"Good visuals. Very moving.
Like the fact it's filmed recently
in a park in Liverpool, but uses
'cine style', which evokes
nostalgia for a lost era of park
use. Serious message at the end
really wrenches you out of your
halcyon daze. Accompanying
explanation was helpful."
Polly Turton – CABE Space

Domenic Lippa

Greatest event: It would have had to be something like the Make Poverty History campaign actually succeeding.

Greatest website: Easy – BBC Online. Maybe I'm getting old, but the news just seems more interesting these days. It's the first thing I look at in the morning when I get in.

Greatest song: Fuck, this is hard. There are just so many – there's a Kylie song I like, and definitely Otis Redding's *I've been loving you too long*, Al Green, Vandross, lots of soul, but at the moment it's probably *Young American* by David Bowie. I was walking around NYC recently, and I was playing it so loud I had to stop, as my heartbeat was just racing!

Greatest painter: I would go for Matisse in 4th, Rothko in 3rd, Ben Nicholson in 2nd but Stuart Davies in 1st. Reminds me of NYC, my family, life, music and everything.

Greatest designing tool: Pencil, pen, paper, Mac are all great, but it has to be the brain. Nothing will happen without it! *Domenic Lippa co-founded Lippa Pearce, a multi-disciplinary graphic design agency based in London*

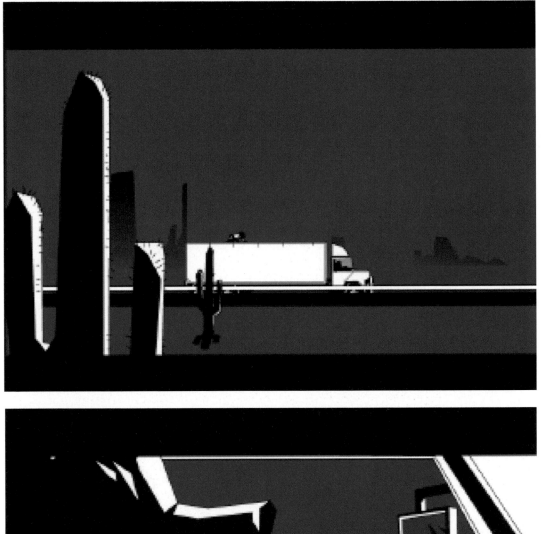

Yaron Peled
Commended
ycn username YARON_PELED
College Ravensbourne
Tutors Liz Friedman and
Penny Hilton
"Really on brief. Cool. Looked
great, sounded great."
Stuart Smith
Wieden and Kennedy

gist

ISSUE 01 2005 | THEME

MEMORY

As seen through the eyes
of English fashion Queen
Vivienne Westwood, a fish
from the North Sea, a New
York poet and a portugese
painter lost in childhood!

VIVIENNE WESTWOOD
FASHIOIN MEMOIR

PAULA REGO'S MAP OF MEMORY
REAL AND IMAGINED STORIES

MEMORY FOOD
THE BRAIN GONE FISHING

LOOKING BACK & MOVING FORWARD
IRAN ON THE VERGE OF REFORM

TELL ME AGAIN
MARA BERGMAN

£ 4.99   € 7.99

8 340 172 95 091 7

www.gistmagazine.co.uk

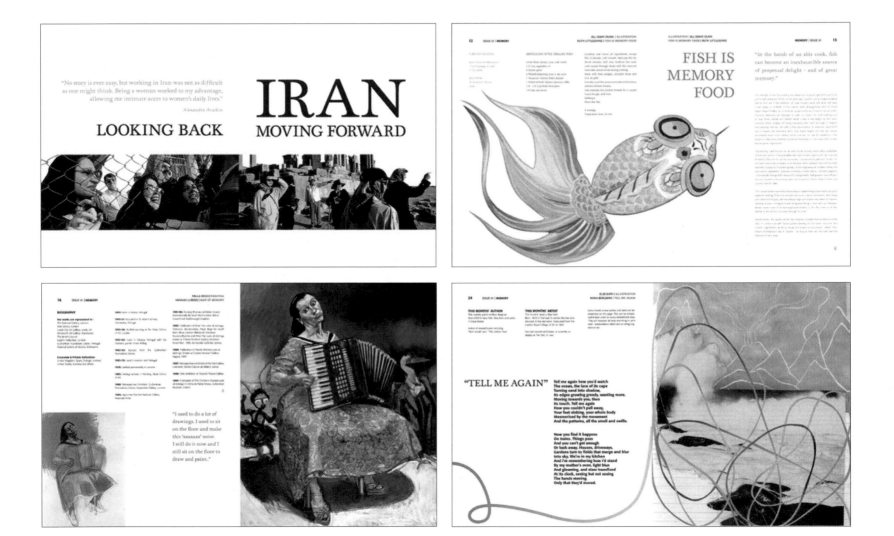

judging rockets

PICTURES BY ANNIE COLLINGE

All work commended as part of the first round of ycn judging is exhibited for invited figures from across the design and advertising industries to view.

Once on display, the judges can decide which submissions are the 'best of year' – and worthy of a Rocket award.

This year, the exhibition was held in July at the Fashion Space Gallery at London College of Fashion. Over the period of a week, people from across the creative industries visited the exhibition to identify the most outstanding work of the year. A full list of all the industry figures that took part in this year's second round of judging can be seen at the ycn website, along with details of the first round of the competition's judging.

Each year, the most popular among all of those commended are declared to be the outstanding submissions of the year, and are presented with a physical award called a Rocket, which last year was designed for ycn by Nick Crosbie at Inflate.

This year there were four such submissions, whose work can be seen in this book. These were; Jonathan Clements (p16–17), Tom White (p90–91) Matt Lewis (p110–111), and Dominic Flannigan (p116–117). They can all be seen with their awards at the front of the book.

Many thanks to Apple for supplying us with the studio equipment on which the best of the year's interactive and moving-image work was displayed. Thanks also to Izabella Bielawska, who designed both this year's certificate of commendation, and the graphics that were used at the exhibition.

Sarah Walsh
ycn Username dollydagger
College University of Leeds
Tutor Mike Sheedy

Packaging

The newly styled Brylcreem range, with colour coordinated product types.

Wax Stick

Waxes & Putties

Moisturiser

Gels

Point of Sale

Counter top display

For display of products at hairdressers, kiosks and smaller retail outlets.

Direct Mail

Mail Shot with gel samples and competition details.

Supermarket Shelf Strip

Chris Chadwick
Commended

ycn username CHADEGG
College University of Teeside
Tutor Mark Freary

"An excellent interpretation of the brief, producing a strong idea that provides the opportunity to showcase the entire range. Beautifully presented."
Sam Cooper – Brylcreem

Instant Coffee Karma

Poppy Wilcox & Lauren Bensted
Commended
ycn usernames POPPYW,
LAURENB1983
College Buckinghamshire
Chilterns University College
Tutor Zelda Malan

"Another humorous approach, boldly using student-focussed images and associations. The notion of 'instant coffee karma' has a nice and campaignable ring to it."
Neil McLeod – Café Direct

Mark Daw & Kooch Chung

Greatest designer:

Mark: Yugo Nakamura. For me it has to be this guy, I love web sites and I have never come across anyone who can weld your attention to the screen like him.

Kooch: Josef Muller Brockmann. He was the type master.

Greatest fairy tale:

Mark: *The Emperor's New Clothes*. I had it as a kid in a brilliantly illustrated book with an audiocassette tape. I never got tired of that one. Plus naked people are funny when you're young.

Kooch: *The Hare and the Tortoise*. It lets me know you shouldn't rush life. Slow and steady wins the race.

Greatest brand:

Mark: Nike. When I was twelve, I remember painting the Nike swoosh logo onto my cricket pads to look like they sponsored me. They have a massive influence and presence, plus their online stuff is ace.

Kooch: Playstation. It takes you to another place, if only for a few minutes.

Greatest job:

Mark: 80s rock star. No more worrying about haircuts, where you're staying tonight or turning your music down.

Kooch: Cat. You get fed and play around with string

Mark and Kooch's work is on page 10.

Matthew Mills
Commended
ycn username GECKODE
College University of Derby
Tutors Tracy Allen-Smith, Leo
Broadley and Gus Hunneybun

"Matthew used the existing jar
and label to good effect with his
mountain window, revealed by
the anarchic rip from students
below."

Neil McLeod – Café Direct

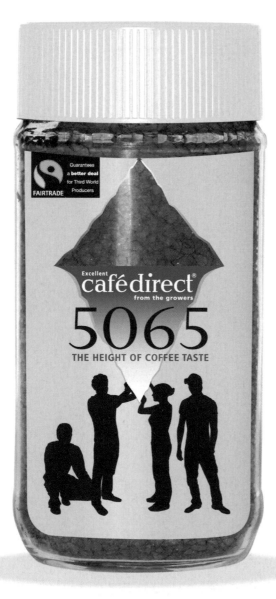

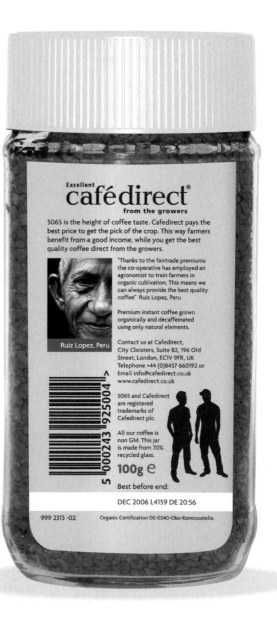

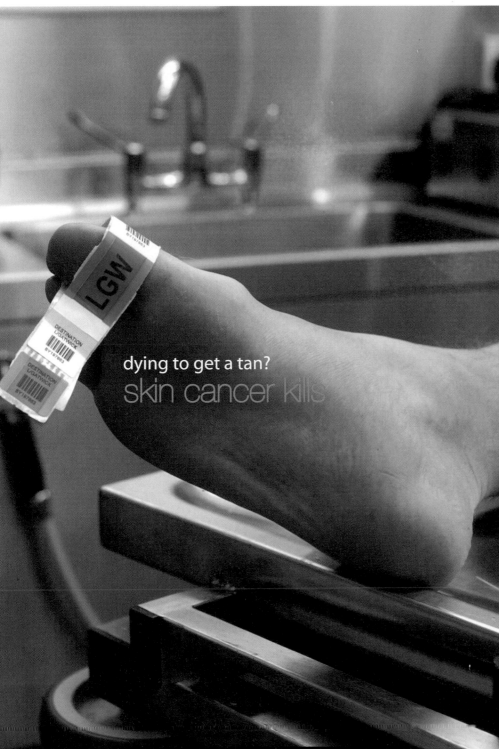

dying to get a tan?
skin cancer kills

LIVE4TODAY.CO.UK

Edward Whatton
Commended
ycn username EDO
College Swindon College
Tutors Greg Rendell and
Pete Benson
"A superbly presented
concept that took a very direct
approach, giving a strong, clear
and powerful message."
Hilary Brailey
Cancer Research UK

design with a conscie. (part one)

BY ADRIAN SHAUGHNESSY

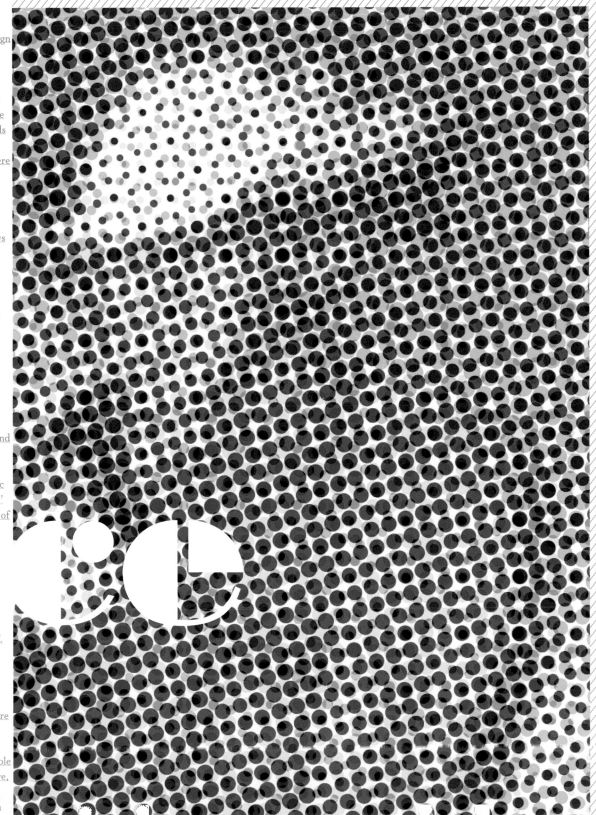

The 1980s saw a boom in the demand for graphic design. Businesses recognised that design and 'style' made their products irresistible to an increasingly affluent and image-obsessed population. For those designers willing to hitch themselves to the business juggernaut, the rewards were considerable: fees were high, work was plentiful and there was a flashy glamour (a first for graphic design) to be gained by being among the shock troops of this new 'loadsamoney' economic revolution. The 1980s was known as the 'designer-decade'.

It was also known as the 'greed-is-good-decade', a revolution as cataclysmic as the industrial revolution. In the technologically advanced West, manufacturing economies became service economies, technology replaced manual labour, and the pursuit of personal wealth replaced older notions of the value of society and community.

Throughout the 1990s, despite the occasional economic recession, the 'upward mobility' (a favourite phrase of the time) of graphic designers continued. This was the era of 'the brand', and branding was the new business panacea. At its most crass, branding 'philosophy' dictated that anything could be made to sell, as long as it was properly and expertly 'branded'. Overnight, graphic designers restyled themselves as 'brand consultants', brand engineers', and more sinisterly, as 'brand guardians'. And for this they were well rewarded.

While most designers accepted, even relished, their role in the new brand-fixated culture, others did not. Many designers questioned their involvement in

it. Many noted that, in the eyes of their clients, design only had a value if it contributed to the sale of consumer goods. Many designers were troubled by the products and companies they were asked to promote – tobacco most famously, but also corporations who ran third-world sweatshops, and even record labels that had subsidiary companies engaged in the manufacture of military weapons.

Others were uneasy about functioning in a culture that used design and advertising as the foremost tools of seduction to lure people into buying goods and services that they often didn't need. They were dismayed to contribute to a culture dependent on waste and disposability. Shopping was the new rationale for existence, and the packaging that goods were sold in, often beautifully designed, was frequently worth more than the goods themselves. Firms and corporations spent more on advertising their products than they did on manufacturing them, thus creating a 'hidden' cost to be borne by the consumer – a 'conspiracy' that designers were implicated in. A small minority of designers felt an urge to put their skills to better use. Rebellion was in the air.

Nor was this the first time that a small group of designers had doubted the wisdom of becoming the shock troops of consumerism. In 1964, the English designer Ken Garland persuaded a group of designers and photographers to sign their names to a manifesto, First Things First. Garland envisaged a more socially beneficial use for designers' talents. He wrote: "We have reached a

saturation point at which the high-pitched scream of consumer selling is no more than sheer noise. We think that there are other things more worth using our skills and experience on. There are signs for streets and buildings, books and periodicals, catalogues, instructional manuals, industrial photography, educational aids, films, television features, scientific and industrial publications, and all other media through which we promote our trade, our education, our culture, and our greater awareness of the world."

Thirty-five years later, Garland's document was adopted and remodelled by a new generation of designers and critics. In the economic and political climate of 1999, when the second First Things First appeared, much of what Garland had envisaged was now an everyday reality. Designers had been sucked into a vortex of frenzied commercial and brand-related activity. Following the oil crises of 1973, opting out and living cheap was no longer an option. In the new post-Thatcher/Reagan world, designers had mortgages, pension schemes and other unavoidable living expenses; and there was a huge cost attached to the mere act of running even a small design studio.

Although the reaction to the second First Things First was intense (pro and anti), and further fuelled by the publication of *No Logo* in 2000, its influence did not extend much beyond the design community. It was dismissed as 'unimaginative Seventies college campus Marxism' by one commentator, and largely ignored by the majority of professional graphic designers. Designers who

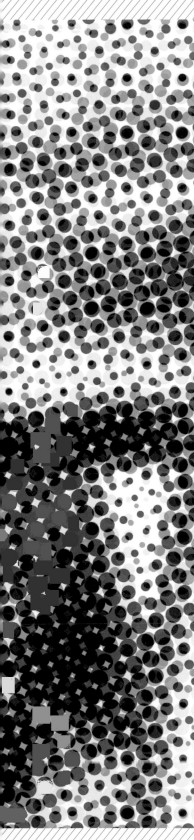

supported the views expressed in First Things First were often made to feel at odds with mainstream design culture. Neville Brody for one believes that designers have a social responsibility:

"I lecture on this constantly and the reaction I usually get is, "all we want to do is design pretty pictures with no thought about social consequences." In my view, designers are public servants. Design is in theory a public service that has come out of the idea that things can be improved by design. But we've become largely a toolbox of commercialism, and more and more we don't care about the people who see our work; we only care about the people who pay for it, and what our peers think about it."

Brody isn't alone. In recent years, a small yet significant number of designers have determined to put their abilities, and experience, to better use. In reality, this usually involves not abandoning commercial work, but developing a mixed approach: designers who wanted to 'give something back' work on commercial projects, but devote a certain amount of time for work that feels like it has some social worth.

Paradoxically, this is easier said than done. In a twist that Garland and his co-signatories could not have envisaged, charities are now run as modern, sexy businesses. They have their own 'brand identities', which they guard with the zeal of any brand-centric corporation. They also demand design that apes, or at least aspires to, the slick qualities of the best consumer-focussed design, and in many cases, prefer the services of big design groups experienced at working with

corporate clients. As the designer Lucienne Roberts, a signatory of the 1999 First Things First manifesto who has worked for many charities, noted in a recent article: "Now I have meetings with communications directors who worked for McDonald's in a previous life, call people who donate money 'clients', and model their strategic thinking on the mass market and mainstream. Yuck. This wasn't what I signed up for."

Roberts' experience is common, but not universal. It is still possible to find institutions and non-profit making bodies who will gladly accept help from designers with a commitment to the cause they stand for. Nor is it any longer embarrassing for designers to admit to doing work with a social value – even some of the bigger design groups now boast about doing a quota of charity work. You could say that 'putting something back' has become cool. It has also never been more necessary.

Adrian Shaughnessy co-founded Intro, where he worked with clients such as PlayStation, Deutsche Bank and the BBC. He now runs This Is Real Art, and writes regularly for Creative Review, Eye *and* Grafik

Lenore Gristwood

Greatest magazine: *Nova*. The art direction by Harri Peccinotti was way ahead of its time. The covers were groundbreaking, and so were the articles - they appealed to both sexes and some dealt with controversial subjects. It didn't last long but it paved the way for future magazines.

Greatest book: *The Alexandria Quartet* by Lawrence Durrell. It's four books, each telling the same story from a different point of view. It introduced me to the darker side of literature, a world peopled by eccentrics and misfits in an exotic and dangerous setting.

Greatest advertisement: *1984* for Apple Macintosh. It was the first time that a time-based ad had all the qualities of cinema. The art direction by Ridley Scott was stunning, and it showed the potential of what can be done in thirty seconds.

Greatest album cover: New Order's *Power, Corruption and Lies* designed by Peter Saville. The image on the cover was Henri Fantin-Latours' Roses, a classical painting, and on the reverse a colour wheel that represented the alphabet in which, if you were so disposed, you could read the message. It was sophisticated, elegant and intelligent - not qualities usually associated with pop music.

Greatest teacher: Nature. Its infinite variety, subtlety, beauty and cruelty. One can only learn from its majesty, yet we are in danger of destroying it through our own greed and ignorance.

Leonore Gristwood is a course leader at Manchester Metropolitan University

Philippa Ip & Sachini Imbuldeniya
Commended
ycn username POI(LIN), SACHI
College Middlesex University
Tutor Phil Healy

"'It's cool to be square' as a line taps into a consumer trend around people wanting to be different in order to fit in. It clearly separates cartons from other formats based on its shape, but perhaps where this isn't as strong as others, is giving this shape a benefit versus other formats.
The packaging images are interesting, and give a feel of something a little bit different."
Chris Trapps – Ribena

Timothy Butler
Commended
ycn username T_M_BUTLER
College De Montfort University
Tutors Ian Newsham and
John Crawford
"Definitely one of the funniest
entries, this campaign showed
people riveted to their television
sets watching such high action
games as Tiddlywinks,
Connect 4, and Jenga.
Very simple, very neat, on
strategy, and a nice evolution
of the 'It matters more when
there's money on it' thought."
Ed Collin – Mother

skybet •Football •Cricket •Connect 4
It Matters More When There's Money On It

one scene...

...never fogotten

CUMBRIA THE LAKE DISTRICT
Brochure Request Line 08705 133059
http://www.golakes.co.uk

Steve Ballinger
Commended
ycn username LEICSBALLBOY
College De Montfort University
Tutors Ian Newsham and
John Crawford
"We all thought this was brilliant
– clever and responded perfectly
to the brief. Love the strapline
'One scene... never forgotten'.
Fantastic idea with reflection in
the glass and the beer mat with
'Cumbria - the Lake District'.
A really versatile and clever
concept."
Penny Watson
Cumbria Tourist Board

Peter Simmons
Commended
ycn username PTSIMMONS
College University College
Falmouth
Tutor John Unwin
"This work demonstrated an
excellent understanding of both
the brief and the mobile market.
The giveaway underwear was a
very nice touch that added value
brilliantly. This was also one of
the few submissions to give
thought to the environmental
issues facing designers (this was
not part of the brief, but
encouraging to see
nevertheless)."
Damian Schnabel
Virgin Mobile

100% PARK

HANDLE WITH CARE

MADE BY MOM

WEAR WITH PRIDE

UNIQUE
DELICATE

**Johanna Mostert
Kuusinen**
ycn username johmo
College Chelsea College of Art
Tutors Pete Maloney
and Tracey Waller

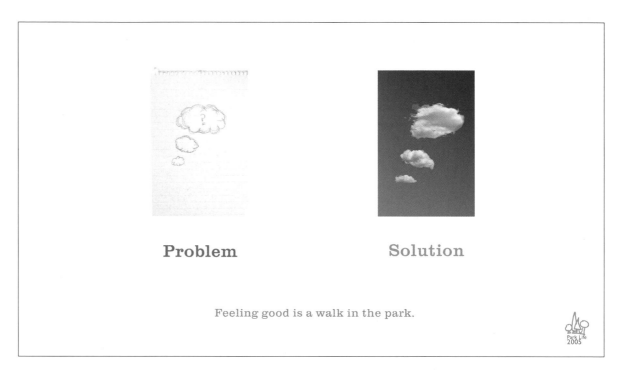

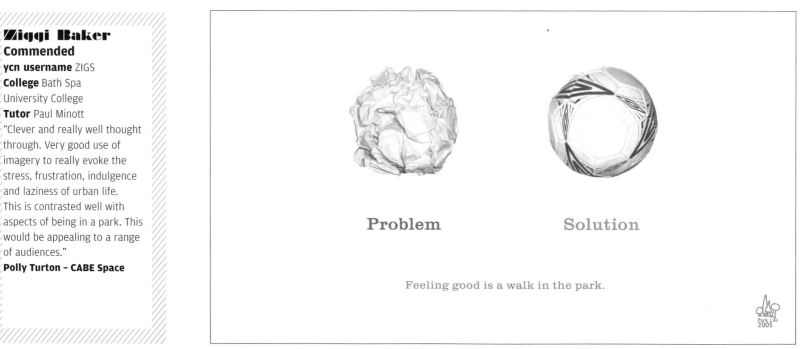

Ziggi Baker
Commended
ycn username ZIGS
College Bath Spa
University College
Tutor Paul Minott
"Clever and really well thought through. Very good use of imagery to really evoke the stress, frustration, indulgence and laziness of urban life. This is contrasted well with aspects of being in a park. This would be appealing to a range of audiences."
Polly Turton – CABE Space

helvetica

Seb Royce

Greatest font: Helvetica Neue Condensed. A cliché but it's simple, clear, can be used anywhere and our website is full of it.

Greatest piece of technology: Turntables. I love collecting vinyl, and of course you need something to play it on. I can spend hours messing around on decks in my house.

Greatest building: Any Huf house. Huf Haus is a German company that creates stunning made-to-order houses from scratch and within a week! German efficiency at its creative best.

Greatest TV programme: *Brass Eye*. Brilliant satire and Chris Morris' finest TV moment. Anyone who can get Phil Collins to wear a hat saying NONCE-SENSE on it while getting him to earnestly spout total rubbish to camera is alright by me.

Greatest artist: Adam Neate. www.adamneate.co.uk Great artist with a graffiti background. Has done loads of street-art exhibitions, and is starting to get the attention he deserves.

Seb Royce is creative director of digital agency Glue London. www.gluelondon.com

Helen Murgatroyd
Commended
ycn username NELEHMURG
College Manchester Metropolitan University
Tutors Sue Platt, Karen Russel and Fiona Small

"Very nice concept. Love the adaptation of the brand and the clean simplicity of the message. May be better with objects that link specifically to the Lake District but would be very keen to persue this style of creative for our corporate branding."

Penny Watson
Cumbria Tourist Board

Ian Berry & James Brown
Commended
ycn username IANBERRY
College Buckinghamshire
Chilterns University College
Tutors Zelda Malan and
Lyndon Mallet

"This campaign focussed on the lengths people will go to, to avoid interruption while having laid a bet. The guys communicated this nicely, knocking through the odd wall and cutting down a dozen or so trees, to have an uninterrupted view. Not that we agree with deforestation, but those darn trees do get in the way now and again. We liked the Anger Mat and the Elasticated Remote holder – good demonstrations of 'it matters more when there's money on it'."
Ed Collin – Mother

Ribena Cartons are kind to the environment

Ribena from Cartons taste nicer

Gary Howe
Commended
ycn username GARYHOWE
College University of Lincoln
Tutors Gyles Lingwood
and Barrie Tullet

"It's the use of the straw without any other carton packaging in sight that we really liked.
It shows that this straw is synonymous with Ribena cartons. This is very powerful, and the use of it in different ways such as the 'mmmm…' is great."
Chris Trapps – Ribena

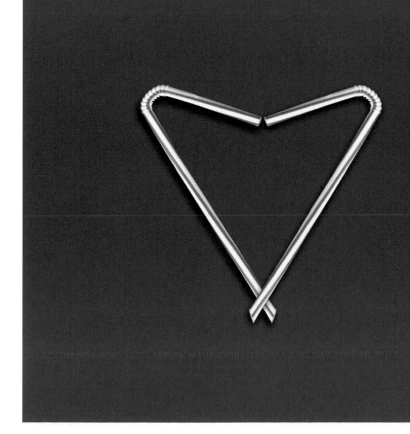

Childhood Sweetheart

THE DIFFERENCE BETWEEN
DRINK
AND
DRUNK
IS
U

TAKE CONTROL

Tom White
Commended
ycn username CHALKY81
College University College Falmouth
Tutors John Unwin, Mark Woodhams and Sue Miller
"This idea captured people's attention because, unlike lots of submissions, it communicates the importance of individual responsibility. In other words, it tells the audience that it's up to them whether they have a great night out. The campaign line is clear, crisp and to the point. We liked the use of the logo, and felt this would help it to become memorable. A bit like 'Think' for road safety."
Kate Blakeley – Diageo

Sonic Youth

Daniel Battams

Greatest brand:
I don't really believe in brands, but the BBC has a better output than most large companies.

Greatest album: Sonic Youth – *Daydream Nation*. Each time I listen to it, something is transferred – a pot boils over, spilling sounds that will stick to various surfaces, and some emotional stuff is recycled in a very special way.

Greatest shop: WH Smiths. Growing up in grim south London, this was a safe haven. I could spend hours in there, looking at magazines, records, games, pens and even books (mainly with pictures).

Greatest item of clothing:
A pair of old H&M jeans. Like most young designers, I am poor; I haven't bought a thing since I graduated two years ago. Thus the remnants of my Camberwell College of Arts wardrobe has a distinct air of The Strokes about it. Graduates: this is a warning. *Daniel Battams runs the Daniel Battams Fan Club Magazine. www.madeupstudios.com*

"do you come here often?"

binge drinking?
you won't impress
them like that

Lucy Gayton
Commended
ycn username LUCYLIU
College University of Lincoln
Tutor Barry Tullet
"The use of gritty images clearly communicated the negative side of binge drinking – who would want to look like that on a night out? The accompanying chat-up lines at first appeared flippant – but when seen alongside the hard-hitting images, clearly weren't. We felt this submission was superb."
Kate Blakeley – Diageo

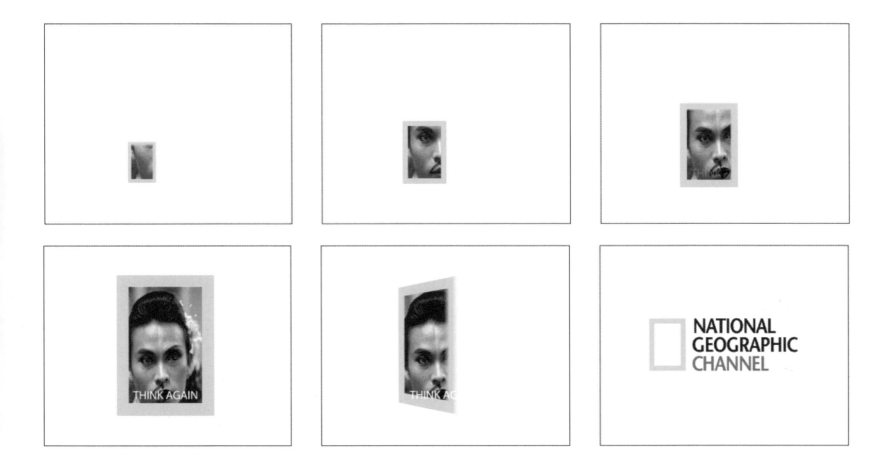

Sebastian Lüer
Commended
ycn username 94907002
College Ravensbourne
College
Tutors Liz Friedman, Ethan
Ames and Penny Hilton

"Wow. A perfectly fitting design
for on-air look, and a very clean
design. This feels very 'Think
Again'."
Justin O'Sullivan
National Geographic Channel

Stuart Palmer
Commended
ycn username
STUARTPALMER01
College Somerset College
of Art and Technology
Tutor Rob Watts

"Good use of urban space, and
would have considerable impact.
Love the idea of demonstrating
the value that proximity to green
space could add to commerical
and residential property."
Polly Turton – CABE Space

perfect placement

BY RICK DODDS & STEPHEN HOWELL
PICTURES BY ANNIE COLLINGE

One day, back in the early summer of 2004, we were sat at our desk at uni, contemplating our work for the final degree show. Rick's mobile rang and it was a number that neither of us recognised. On answering it, we were told the news that we'd won a ycn award – including a cash prize and a creative placement at Saatchi & Saatchi. We leapt from our chairs and ran to the pub.

We graduated from uni each with a first-class degree in BA(Hons) Graphic Design and Advertising, leaving with a couple of great placements to keep us busy for the next few months. We moved into central London and began the struggle of trying to crack into the impenetrable advertising industry. And though we were starting our placements, we knew that to get an actual job was going to take more than our Yorkshire charm.

The placements went well, but we soon realised that three years of uni was only the beginning of learning our trade. We realised there was a massive step up to be made – and found it tough making it. The hardest part of the placements was wondering whether we were still going to be there the following week, whether they were going to hire us or whether a little mistake we made in a review was going to be the end of our short careers. The hours we were working were ridiculous, and the stress and pressure we were feeling often made us question what the hell we were getting ourselves into – but we kept going, because the highs always outweighed the lows.

Seven months later and, after our placements had finished, we found ourselves working in bars, struggling to pay the rent and with no placement in sight. We

phoned ycn and the people there arranged our placement at Saatchi & Saatchi. The big day arrived and we were greeted at Saatchi's by the lovely Tracy Flaherty, who showed us round and helped us settle in. We were soon working on a live brief for a major global brand, and we worked as hard as we could until it was time to start the bar jobs at night. We did well and the team overseeing the work was enthusiastic and approachable – encouraging for a nervous placement team.

We worked on the brief for a week and by the end of the placement, we had work going to the client. Dave Dawkins, the Creative Operations Director, said, "Do you know when you're having a good day? Well it just got better. How's a month's paid extension sound?"

We were chuffed to bits, but then it got better still: "Here's a bottle from the boss."

The expensive bottle of bubbly hit the table nearly as quickly as we then drank it, topping off a fantastic two weeks.

Over the next month, we worked on many of the best briefs in the agency – while working for some of the best creative directors we'd ever met. They kept pushing us to do better, while teaching us along the way, improving both our confidence and our work, all the time. We listened closely to what they said, making notes in every meeting, and simply worked as hard as we could. By the end of the month, we already had some press ads published and were working on pan-European TV briefs, which were big briefs for a placement team to work on.

The end of the month came and we were extended for another month, much to our delight. We

were enjoying Saatchi's more than any other placement we'd done, and found ourselves waking up in the morning and being excited about going to work, which was a very strange feeling that we'd never felt before. One of the best things about Saatchi's is the social side of it, especially getting drunk in the Pregnant Man pub – the agency's own personal watering hole. Everyone is friendly and welcoming, and it wasn't long before we were getting drunk with the vast majority of people who worked at Saatchi & Saatchi.

The second month flew past and we continued to work on pan-European briefs. By the end of the month, we were called into the office of the Executive Creative Director, Kate Stanners. She was fantastic and offered us permanent jobs, changing our lives in one simple sentence. We'll never forget that day and especially our Mums bursting into tears as we told them the day we'd been waiting for, for four years, had finally arrived. That night, we got as drunk as we possibly could, and kept punching the air with delight while uttering the word "Yeesss!" several hundred times.

The last year of our lives had many ups and downs, and we had felt like quitting dozens of times. But, as a good Northern lad once said to us: "Our scars make us who we are." We had finally got the jobs we'd always wanted, but now the hard work really begins.

X-MEN

Ted Hart

Greatest hairstyle: Imagine the "Flock of Seagulls" (like the wings on Thor's helmet, but made of hair), ginger, and on a back-row forward who looks a bit like Wayne Rooney. I knew this man at uni, I swear it.

Greatest film: *The Apartment.* Funny, sad and cool, all at the same time.

Greatest website: Google. Mostly because of its cheesy logo variations, but it does find stuff quickly too.

Greatest publication: *X-men #137.*

Ted Hart is head of UK marketing at Clarks Shoes.

Is it time to re-think your Beans?

Excellent
café**direct**®
from the growers

5065
THE HEIGHT OF COFFEE TASTE

FAIRTRADE
Guarantees
a **better deal**
for Third World
Producers

Colin Fan
Commended
ycn username COLANDE
College UWIC
Tutor Olwen Moseley
"Classic student imagery and associations played on effectively. Nice and simple, which can often be the very best route."
Neil McLeod – Café Direct

Ellen Mitchell
ycn username elsbel
College Bath Spa
University College
Tutor Jack Gardner

FEELING STRESSED?

GETTY IMAGES

Coralie Hartigan
Commended
ycn username CJUK84
College University College Falmouth
Tutors Mark Woodhams and Andy Neil
"Simple and powerful messages. The process of unravelling and repeating the message gradually is very clever."
Polly Turton – CABE Space

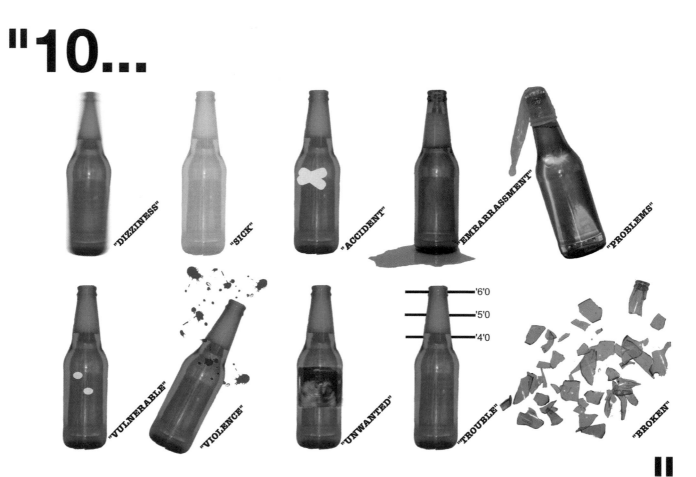

"10...

"DIZZINESS" "SICK" "ACCIDENT" "EMBARRASSMENT" "PROBLEMS"

"VULNERABLE" "VIOLENCE" "UNWANTED" "TROUBLE" "BROKEN"

'6'0 '5'0 '4'0

... REASONS TO CALL LAST ORDERS ON BINGE DRINKING"

Nicholas Newbury
Commended
ycn username NEWBS
College University of Derby
Tutors Helen Neil and
Leo Broadley
"This is an intelligent campaign,
and quite arresting. The words
and images combine to create
something very real. People felt
they could imagine the words
being read out or sung.
The creative idea clearly
communicated the consequences
of drinking excessively. Its hard-
hitting nature was thought to get
the message across very well."
Kate Blakeley – Diageo

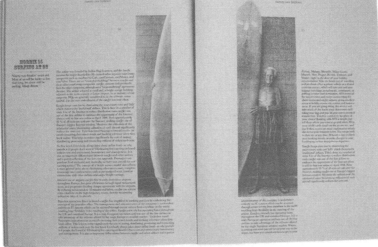

Matt Smith
ycn username m_smith
College University of Lincoln
Tutors Philippa Wood
and Chris Dunne

Matthew Turrell
Commended
ycn username CHEESE
College Stockport College
Tutors Melanie Levick-Parkin
and Leonie Clements

"'You Just Can't Hide It' was a really strong idea that could be executed in a number of different media. Concept shows good understanding of the target audience, using a good blend of style, value and humour."

Sam Cooper – Brylcreem

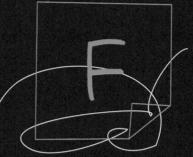

Joamne Greenhalgh

Greatest magazine:
Like most designers, I am a visual surfer. I collect print with a passion (just for the smell of fresh print!), and I love magazines that break editorial/typographical rules. There are so many great experimental, inspirational magazines, such as *d'side*, *Foil*, *Flux*, *Amelia's magazine*, *Rant*.

Greatest phrase:
Don't take life too seriously. Find something in life you love, and be passionate about it!

Greatest cartoonist:
Dr Seuss has inspired me from when I was a child, with his original style and witty characters and stories. I love the organic style of his illustrations, and how well they translate into animation/film.

Greatest drawing instrument:
Anything that makes a mark! Some of the best typography I've seen include bits of impromptu signs /messages left on Post-its, chalked on walls, drawn on Etch-a-Sketch.

Greatest font:
I often go back to Helvetica for its versatility and simplicity. But it's not the font, it's what you do with it.

Joanne Greenhalgh is a tutor at City College Manchester

Andrew Cheung
Commended
ycn username ZUSUN83
College Loughborough University
Tutor Anne Brooks

"Broad and in-depth exploration to keep students awake. Good logo device in the word 'up'. The strength of the idea got slightly diluted, but some nice reference to student life and vices, such as using a drinks optic to dispense product."
Neil McLeod – Café Direct

Take care when spending time in the sun, try to cover up and use a factor 15 or higher.

TODAY Is raising money to fight cancer and supports cancer research

SunSmart

Registered charity number: 1089464

Matt Lewis
Commended
ycn username DINGEROUS
College Liverpool John
Moores University
Tutor Johnathan Hitchen
"A really great concept that
challenges the traditional
format and layout of magazines.
It's a brave and refreshing
approach that combines
good design with excellent
typography. It also has a very
mature sense of pace, including
a typographic section just using
an excellent string-like font.
Not all of us were convinced that
the elderly audience would 'get
it' – but hey, you can't have
everything."
Chris Parker – JBCP

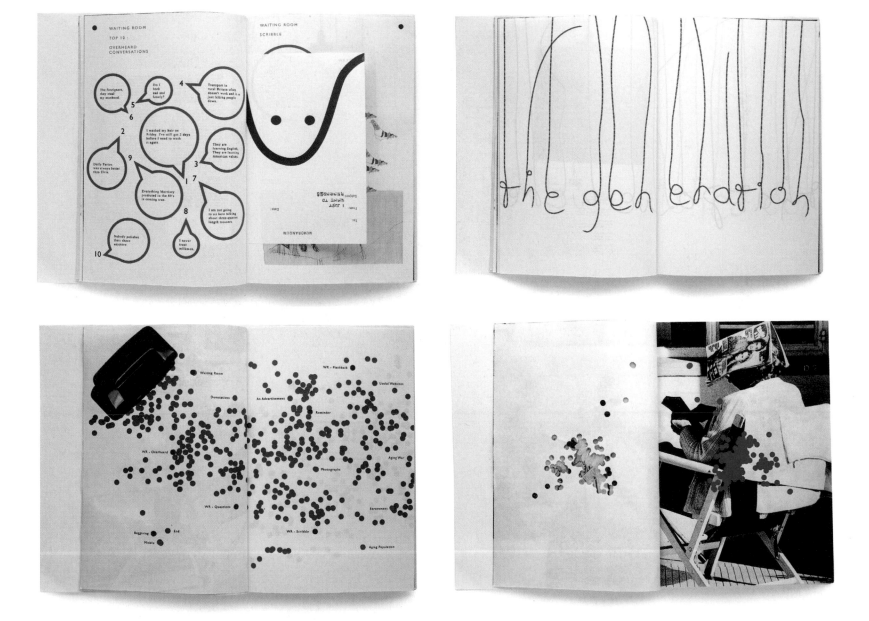

Bryan Edmondson

Greatest website:
www.showstudio.com
Must see is the 'forget me not'
project by Julie Verhoeven and
Peter Saville.

Greatest product: I love
furniture, so maybe Fred Scott's
Supporto chair. These are what
we sit on at SEA.

Greatest book: Fabian Baron's
book with Madonna, *SEX.* I was
a student when I first saw this,
and the copy and photography
are still amazing. It was also
the first piece of Fabian Baron's
work I saw.

Greatest photograph: *The
Cowboy Series* by
Richard Prince.

Greatest architect:
Tadoa Ando, because of his
Church of Light.
*Bryan Edmondson is one of the
founders of SEA Design.*
www.seadesign.co.uk

STYLE
IRRESISTIBLE CHARM

STYLE
REPULSIVELY
CHARMLESS

Vicky Young
Commended
ycn username VIXS53
College University College
Falmouth
Tutors Mark Woodhams
and Andy Neil
"We loved this creative idea – it
was an unusual, refreshing take
on the brief, and showed a really
clever way to use traditional
media. We liked the fact that
the first page could almost go
unnoticed, yet when you turn
over, there's the element of
surprise. The idea was brilliantly
executed, with real care over the
casting, wardrobe and lighting.

The detail given to how the
models morph – the changes to
their posture, expressions, etc –
was really impressive.
We anticipated this idea could
work well with both women's
and men's lifestyle magazines."
Kate Blakeley – Diageo

Lucie Raufast
ycn username lucieraufast
College Chelsea College of Art
Tutors Pete Maloney and
Tracey Waller

Visit your local park

Nicole Trinder
Commended
ycn username 1207NICOLE
College Swindon College
Tutors Greg Rendell and
Mike O'Brian

"The 'Impossible' concept really appealed to us, and was clearly well thought through."
Justin O'Sullivan
National Geographic Channel

Anthony and Cleopatra are found lying dead in their Egyptian hideaway.

Nearby is a broken bowl.

There were no marks on their bodies.

They were not poisoned.

How did they die?

How did they die?
Egypt Detectives
Sunday 9pm

Impossible.

Think Again.

Press Yellow ☐ Now.

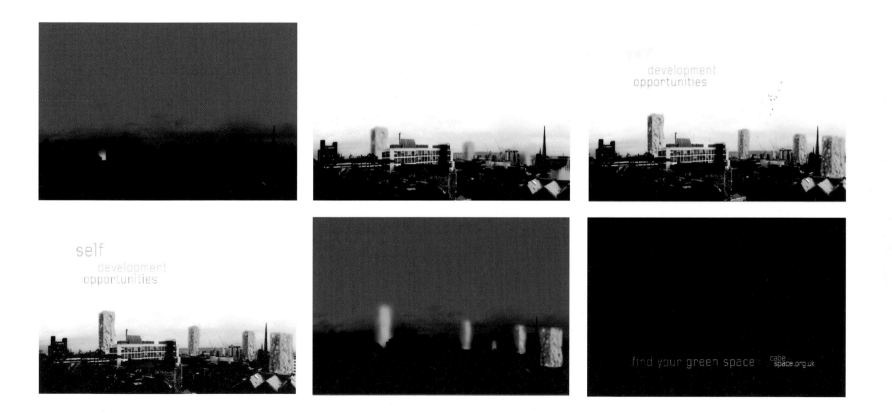

**Dominic
Flannigan**
Commended
ycn username SUMWON
College Glasgow School of Art
Tutors Steve Rigley and Jo Petty

"A combination of the practical
and the inspirational. A mixture
of reality and 3D visualisation is
good, and this work emphasises
parks as part of the fabric of the
city." **Polly Turton – CABE Space**

design with a conscie (PART TWO)

BY JAMES HAMILTON

Advertising and altruism; not two words commonly uttered in the same room, let alone the same breath. Ethics? They're for people who work in the public sector; they'd only get in the way on a multi-million pound marketing push.

Graphic design and advertising agencies are acutely aware of this image problem. Both industries spend a good deal of time and effort attempting to disprove it. Cynics might label their efforts "tokenism"; an attempt to spin the negative impressions these companies have earned in a society that is growing increasingly hostile to brand building and marketing. But that's to do them an injustice. Most agencies and studios will have at least one charity client, and while some of them charge for their services on these accounts, a vast proportion of the work they do is pro bono. Gratis. Free.

Perhaps the most famous of the agencies-with-a-heart is St Lukes. Founded in the '90s with an overtly ethical company credo, the London-based advertising agency prides itself on both the amount it gives back to the voluntary sector, and the range of causes it works with.

"We allow everyone 50 hours a year to work on non-billing work," explains the St Lukes joint managing director, Neil Henderson. "People can work with whatever cause they like – we have people who help out at a local school, for example." Mostly, staff work on charity campaigns.

Currently, St Lukes is doing work for Greenpeace and Tourism Concern. St Lukes is also a carbon-neutral agency: it calculates the amount of CO_2 its business creates and plants trees to counteract the environmental impact. Bless.

"The main reason we do pro bono work for charities is, first and foremost, because people in the agency want to help support good causes. Charities are involved in serious and often emotional issues, and advertising can play an important part in their success – not just in the awareness it creates for the cause, but also creating a focus for their activity," says Henderson, pointing out that there are clear benefits for the agency working on pro bono charity campaigns: free from the pressure that making money creates, creative teams get a chance to be more autonomous- a useful tool when training juniors.

Lucy Unger, managing partner at the London office of the international design studio Fitch, agrees: "Creative teams in design studios are tightly structured in terms of hierarchy. Pro bono work is a really good training ground for middleweight designers to take ownership of a project."

Rodney Fitch, the founder of Fitch, has made it his stated aim that every studio in the Fitch network carry out at least one pro bono project a year. The London studio has worked in the past creating publicity material for the charity Alone In London. This year, it is taking a different slant, asking each of its 50 designers to create a t-shirt that will be printed up and sold, with all the proceeds going to an as-yet-undecided charity.

Pro bono work offers more than simply an opportunity to give less experienced staff a taste of face-to-face dealings with clients. There's the more nebulous 'contentment' factor to

LOST GORILLA

Last seen in the African rainforest. Disappeared from his home shortly after it was illegally chopped down to make garden furniture. Will answer to the name "EXTINCT"

CONTACT: Your local garden centre, to check the furniture they sell carries the Forest Stewardship Council logo.

REWARD: Saving an endangered species.

take into account, too. At Abbott Mead Vickers BBDO (an agency with a long list of pro bono clients, including The Royal Ballet, The Type Museum and, most recently, the Make Poverty History initiative), a staff survey showed a broad groundswell of approval for the agency's Big House project, a three-year fundraising project to buy a house to help the long-term homeless off the streets. Says George Bryant, the head of planning at AMV BBDO: "There are clear benefits, both from an ethical and business perspective, to working with charitable organisations on a pro bono basis. Involvement with these organisations might not always bring a direct benefit to the bottom line, but it presents agencies with an important opportunity to demonstrate their beliefs, values and creative strengths."

There are those, though, that dispute the value of the "something for nothing" equation that pro bono work provides for charities and not-for-profit organisations, voicing real concerns that such arrangements might not be in the charities' best interests.

"When a charity works with an above-the-line agency, whether it is paying for the work or getting it for free, what they are 'buying' is usually profile or awareness," says Stephen Butler, the director of Domain, an advertising agency that works exclusively with charity clients.

"When they work with a specialist agency, what they are buying is present and future income. That's a better use of charity funds, which, after all, are donated money," he says.

Holly Dyer, the co-founder of Bananadesign, a charity-focussed design studio, argues that the same is true for design work: "Problems can arise when charities expect work to be done for free, or when the studio doesn't put as much effort into a free piece of work as a paid piece." She also cites the potential minefield of conflicts of interest- a charity working with a design or advertising agency that has clients that do not share the same ethical concerns. "Charities are obviously appreciative of free work, and may not look into this aspect too closely. We've seen this happen a number of times," says Dyer.

AMV BBDO recently created the "jo@samaritans.org" campaign for The Samaritans. Jeremy Payne, the charity's director of fundraising and external affairs, explains the choice of agency: "The brief was very simple and easy to convey, which meant that we could have worked with any number of agencies. The issue of pro bono or not is almost more important than the type of the agency – the nature of the beast is that, if a major client has urgent needs, pro bono work is the first area to slide. If charities can live with this, that's fine, but if they're working on an integrated campaign where timing is critical, losing one element could undermine the whole campaign."

Most agencies and studios will freely admit that paying clients are their first and foremost priority, and get their attention over and above their pro bono accounts. They are also aware of their strengths and limitations, and wouldn't recommend a charity client use them alone.

Agencies like Domain or a studio like Bananadesign can work well alongside pro bono work with a "name" agency.

Take the NSPCC, for instance. The charity has held a paying account with Saatchi & Saatchi for 26 years – one of the agency's longest-running accounts. But that doesn't stop the charity working with a number of different studios and agencies on various parts of its account.

"The NSPCC has a group of agencies. We do awareness work. We all know the areas we're good at," says Kate Stanners, the Saatchi & Saatchi creative director. "It's all about the right skill set – we don't do direct response work; the NSPCC choose us to mastermind their campaigns, we give them something they can use to start fundraising."

And do advertising and design do enough to help charities reach their audience? Jeremy Payne at AMV BBDO says it's hard to tell. "Maybe our industry could come up with its own version of the 'Percent Club'," he says, referring to the Business in the Community-developed scheme scheme where companies benchmark their charitable support with a target of 1 per cent of UK pre-tax profit. "But commercial reality will ensure that companies don't do so much that they damage their own businesses."

James Hamilton is World/Work editor of Campaign *magazine*

Abused children can't speak up.

ABBEY ROAD NW8
CITY OF WESTMINSTER

Lucy Gayton

Greatest object: The Dyson vacuum. Form follows function, it works well and looks cool. Love the funky colours!

Greatest album cover: Abbey Road by The Beatles. The photograph seems to capture the mood of the group at that time in their career.

Greatest magazine: *fact*, an underground music mag. It's full of upcoming, new talent, but I pick it up because the covers look fab, the design has a nice rough, photocopied feel to it, and it's free!

Greatest clothing: Jeans. Where would we be without them? Everyone owns at least one pair – they're comfy, and you can wear them with virtually anything!

Greatest charity: The NSPCC. Its message is strong and direct, its campaigning brings the awful truth of what goes on behind close doors to light. The NSPCC is the voice of thousands of neglected and ill-treated children.
Lucy's work is on page 93.

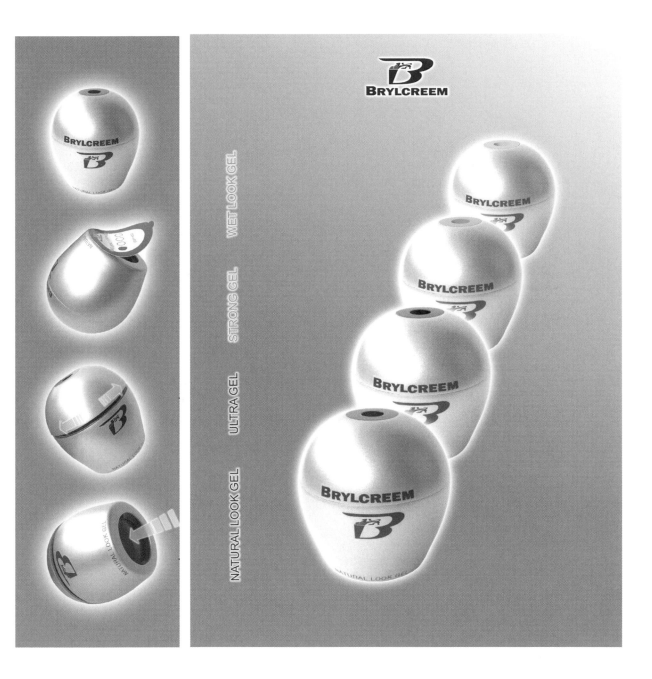

Li Jiang
Commended
ycn Username LJIANG
College Sheffield Hallam
University
Tutors Claire Lockwood,
Glyn Hawley and Bill Stewart
"A strong gel-dispensing idea –
innovative and different to
most of the offerings already
on the market."
Sam Cooper – Brylcreem

Martyn Shouler
Commended

ycn username SHOULER
College University of Luton
Tutors Nick Jeeves, Tim Metcalf
and Ed D'Souza

"A really strong and
contemporary concept. The
'doodley' style was universally
loved during the judging, and
gives real scope for flexibility.
We thought that the strapline
worked really well here."
Penny Watson
Cumbria Tourist Board

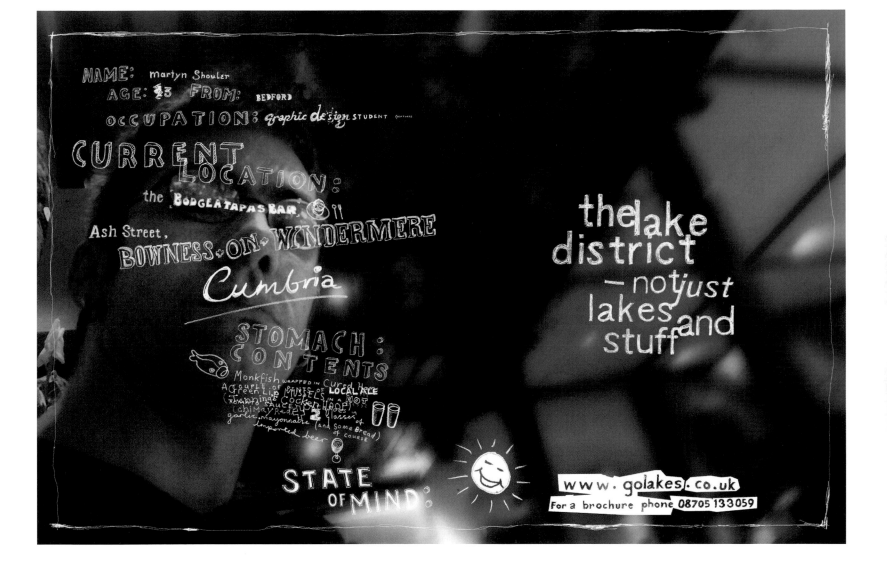

**Oli Kellet &
Alex Holder**
Commended
ycn username OLIALEX
College Central St Martins
Tutors Clive Challis, Maggie
Souter and Zelda Malan
"Very simple and strong ideas."
Justin O'Sullivan
National Geographic Channel

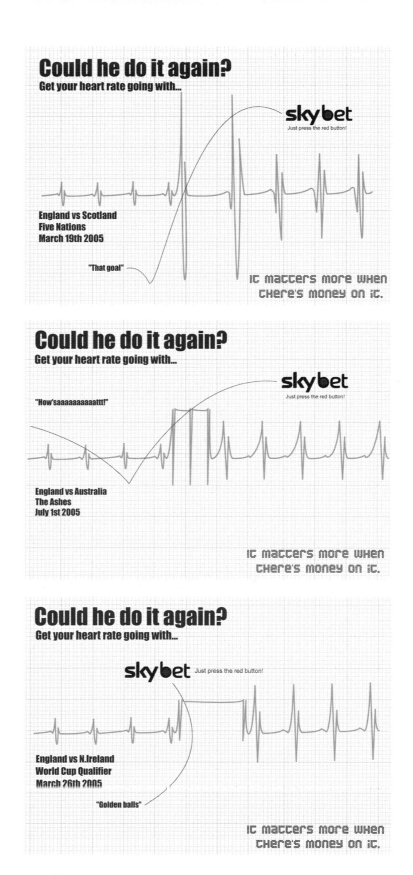

Robert Garner
Commended
ycn username ROB_GARNER
College University of Derby
Tutors Gus Hunneybun,
Helen Neil, Tracy Allen-Smith
and Leo Broadley

Matt Gardner
ycn username tdotuk
College Southampton Institute
Tutor Steve Lannin

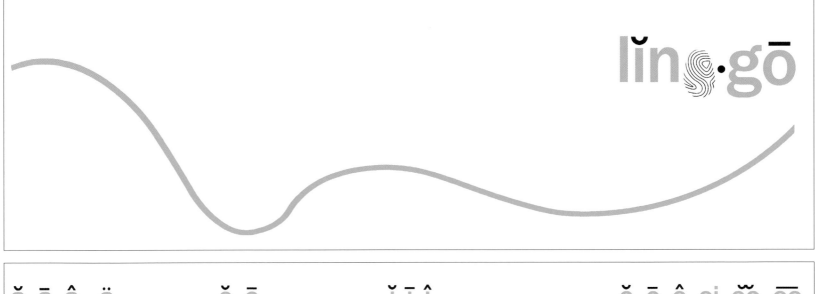

lĭn**•**gō

ă	ā	âr	ä	b	c	ch	ĕ	ē	f	g	h	hw	ĭ	ī	î	r	j	k	l	m	n	ng	ŏ ō ô oi oo̅ oō̅

pat pay care father   bitch pet bee   which pĭt plē plēr   thing pŏt tōe hôrse noise took boot

ou̅ p r s h t th *th* ŭ û̅r v w x y z   ə ər wĕl•kəm

out   tate thin that cut urge   circus butter syllable

The youth market uses their mobiles equally for text messaging and calls with the majority of minutes used for chatting to friends and texting the latest arrangements. The concept for ling.go is based on the spoken language using phonetic spelling and symbols as a naming system for the phones and any other titles used on brand packaging, point of sale, advertising etc... This creates names that intrigue and stand-out to the consumer. Although not instantly recognisable to all, this would be a benefit as it will result in differences of pronunciation which will give the all-knowing owner a feeling of prestige, for being part of a community not understood by the outside world which would appeal to those seeking to be different. Yet with the majority of the 16-24 age range being in education and with internet access, I believe the phonetic will be recognisable if only sub-consciously from the use of online dictionaries where the phonetic spelling is given in any search result. Once understood that the phone names are spelt as they are spoken it is a very simple language to understand. The phonetic symbols used to highlight vowels also were used on packaging as part of the brands visual identity.

The brand name 'lingo' straight away implies a "specialist vocabulary and characteristic language of a particular group", setting the owner apart from other mobile users. Do you speak the ling.go?

the spoken language

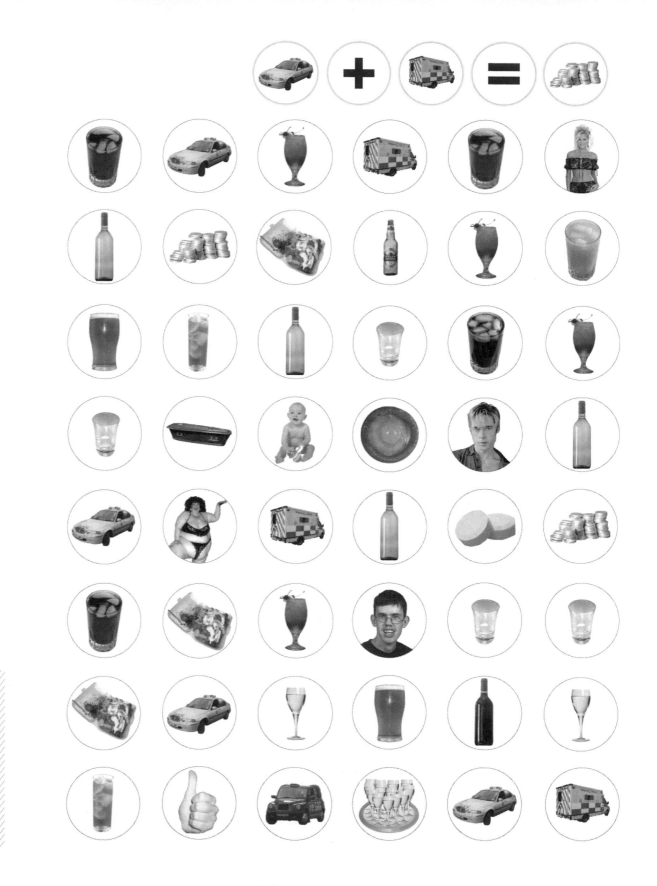

Vincent Howcutt
ycn username chenz
College The Arts Institute
at Bournemouth
Tutors Roger Gould
and Martin Coyne

Clare Prior

Greatest colour: White. I look forward to a day when I can have more of it in my life without spilling.

Advertisement: The '3' ad where the Japanese cowboys take home the giant jellyfish. Leon Jaume told us that the idea was simple – it was just meeting a girl and taking her home for a drink and a dance. The madness cracks me up.

Greatest packaging design: Matthew Williamson's Coke bottles. A friend has them on the windowsill at work, and I never get tired of admiring them.

Greatest album cover: The Sugarcubes *Life's Too Good* (designed by Paul White at the Me Company). How can you argue with an album that came in 5 different day-glo colours? Treasured from my youth, I love the neon orange and simple design – a reminder of a fantastic era.

Greatest fashion designer: Coco Chanel. An amazing woman and a legend in design. *Clare Prior is a strategist at Ingram.*

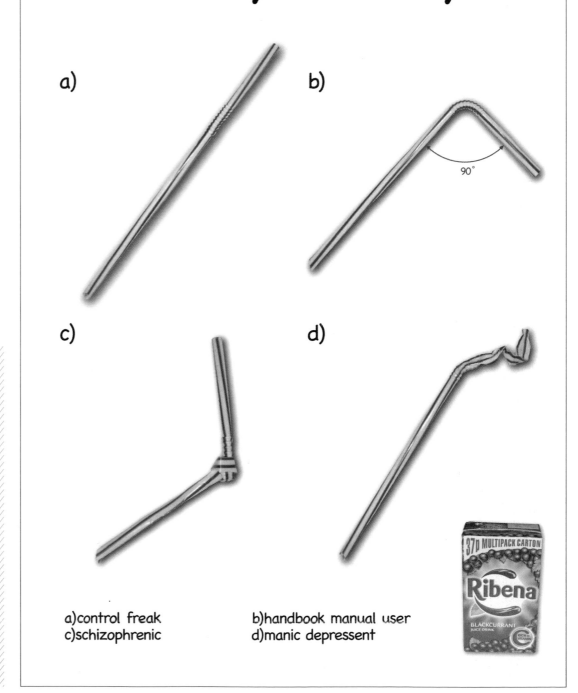

What does your straw say about you?

a)

b)

90°

c)

d)

a)control freak
c)schizophrenic

b)handbook manual user
d)manic depressent

Sarah Roberts
Commended
ycn username SROBERTS
College Swindon College
Tutor Pete Benson
"This gave the carton a reason to stand out versus other packaging formats. This entry turns the straw into something which is relevant for the adult audience. The fact that it can be used (or used to say something about the person) adds an element of personability to the consumer, something we have seen to be relevant for the young adult audience."
Chris Trapps – Ribena

Join us

www.iee.org

There are a number of ways you can register your interest:

○ E-mail businesspartners@iee.org.uk. Simply head your e-mail Business Partners

Application and a form will be sent to you by return.

○ Fax us on +44 (0) 1438 767305 requesting an Application form which can then Be faxed or mailed back to you.

○ On line. [26KB MS Word Document]

○ Partnership is open to all companies and organisations with an interest in the work of the IEE.

○ Partners are encouraged to nominate an appropriate point of contact within their organisation to act as the main contact with the IEE.

○ Membership is free: there is no annual fee to become a Business Partner.

Further details are available from:

IEE Business Partners
Michael Faraday House
Six Hills Way
Stevenage
Herts
SG! 2AY

Tel :+44 (0) 1438 767392
Fax:+44 (0) 1438 742856
Email: businesspartners@iee.org

Navigation menu (repeated on each screen):
What does the iee do?
What is the Business Partners initiative?
Why are we offering you this partnership?
How will being a member benefit your company?
Join us
Contacts

Why are we offering you this partnership?

www.iee.org

The IEE believes that it shares with industry powerful common ambitions and concepts:-

○ The development and promotion of technical competence in individuals which benefit the companies for whom they work as well as industry and society as a whole.

○ The creation and maintenance of a professional community in which commercial enterprises play a key part.

○ The provision of events and activities where companies can converse informally yet meaningfully about shared interests. A relaxed network, yet one which can often spark inspiration and drive initiative and enterprise.

In pursuit of these aims, the IEE provides a well-developed range of products and services of value to industry, all of which are presented via IEE Business Partners.

In an age when virtually every company relies on electrical products and electronic services to do business, electrical engineers and electronics technologists are not only vital to engineering companies, but also increasingly to companies where engineering is not the major activity. Working in many different disciplines, these professionals will help determine the competitive fortunes of most organisations.

What is the Business Partners initiative?

www.iee.org

Founded in 1871, the Institution of Electrical Engineers is a not for profit organisation, registered as a charity in the UK.
The goal of the IEE is to develop the electrical engineering and ICT professions in partnership with industry. The IEE Business Partners Programme has been designed as a forum to help us achieve this goal.
There is no fee to pay when a company registers as an IEE Business Partner. Instead you and your company commit to working alongside the IEE to enhance the future of electrical engineering and associated professions.

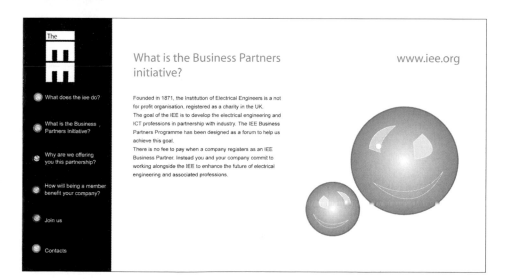

Sarah Blackmore
Commended
ycn username
SARAH-BLACKMORE
College Loughborough University
Tutors Anne Brooks, Simon Downs and Lorenzo Madge

"Well presented visually with a good supporting concept rational and a very well-produced, fully-working mockup of the CD-Rom. We thought that the use of branding, typography and adherance to the corporate palette were absolutely spot on. Even though, as a brand, we try to avoid wires and circuits imagery, as we cover many diverse industry sectors, the concept of the lines/map network is a good analogy of business partners, and could be visually applied to different sectors of the organisation."

Patrick Cadona – IEE

Andy Altman

Greatest drawing: Drawings by my eldest son, Eddy, aged 5. He had shown absolutely no interest in drawing, but suddenly could not stop drawing strange-looking monsters. 30 drawings in one sitting!

Greatest album cover: All the Top of the Pops album covers from the 70s. All the songs were dreadful cover versions, and the printed covers were incredibly naff – always with a semi-clad girl in costume.

Greatest film: *My Life as a Dog*. Just a beautiful film.

Greatest website: I hate websites!

Greatest shop: ebay. I love it. All the crap you could ever want to own. Where else can you find a George Best jam jar lid?

Andy Altman is one of the founders of Why Not Associates.

phone
fax
mail
visit

0141 Design
0141 440 7241
www.0141design.co.uk
38 Carmunnock Road,
Glasgow G44 4UE

2 Heads
01491 681061
www.2heads.tv
Kit Lane, Checkendon,
Oxfordshire RG8 0TY
Suzanne Elliot

20/20
020 7383 7071
www.20.20.co.uk
20-23 Mandela Street,
London NW1 0DU
Tracy Cheung

23red
0870 0130023
www.23red.com
2nd Floor, Elsley Court,
20/22 Great Titchfield Street,
London W1W 8BE
Philippa Dunning

2AM Design
01772 686222
www.2amdesign.co.uk
The Loft, Mill Farm,
Fleetwood Road,
Wesham PR4 3HD
Peter Stubbs

3 Minds
01922 626321
www.3minds.co.uk
10 Ravensdale Close, Walsall,
West Midlands WS5 3PY
Mike Holloway

3d Canvas
01628 627678
www.3dcanvas.co.uk
havelock Business Park,
Havelock Road, Maidenhead,
Berkshire SL6 5FH
Ollie Lebrocq

400 Communications
020 7404 1114
www.400.co.uk
57 Hatton Garden,
London EC1N 8HP
Paul Dennis / Alicia O'Dell

422 South
01179 467222
www.422south.com
St. John's Court, Whiteladies
Road, Bristol BS8 2QV Janet
Turner

44 Media
0161 278 2059
www.44media.com
38 John Dalton St.,
Manchester M2 6LE
Ty Abiodun

999 Design Group
020 7739 3945
www.999design.co.uk
91/93 Great Eastern Street,
Shoreditch, London EC2A 3HZ
Aileen Geraghty

A&Z Design
020 8365 9136
www.azdesign.co.uk
Unit 7, The Stonebridge Centre,
Rangemoor Road, Tottenham,
London N15 4LP
Albert Saint Catherine

Abacus e-media
020 7297 5200
www.abacusemedia.com
84-86 Regent Street,
London W1B 5AJ
Steve Feigen

Absolute.Design
01326 316372
www.absolutedesign.co.uk
1st Floor, Post Office, The Moor,
Falmouth, Cornwall TR11 3RB
Helen Blake

AD Creative Consultants
020 8870 8743
www.adcreative.co.uk
The Royal Victoria,
Patriotic Building, Trinity Road,
London SW18 3SX
John Graham

Alembic
020 7288 4580
www.alembic.co.uk
1 Hanover yard, Noel Road,
London N1 8YA
Jonathan Miller

Allen International
020 7371 2447
www.allen-international.com
Berghem Mews, Blythe Road,
London W14 0HN
Dean Neil

Antidote
020 7240 7272
www.antidote.co.uk
24 Litchfield Street,
London WC2H 9HJ
Chris Williams

Arnold Interactive
020 7908 2700
www.arnoldinteractive.com
14 Welbeck Street,
London W1G 9XU
Brian Frakes

Artantica
01277 890418
www.artantica.co.uk
2 Brookside Cottages,
Magdalen Laver, Ongar,
Essex CM5 0EG

Aspect Group
020 7504 6900
www.aspectgroup.co.uk
Clerkenwell House,
67 Clerkenwell Road,
London EC1R 5BL
Jannick Jensen

Astill Associates
0161 237 1799
www.astillassociates.com
3rd Floor, 24 Lever Street,
Stevenson Square,
Manchester M1 1DW
Neil Nisbet

Astound
020 8871 9066
www.astoundingfish.net
1st Floor, Jessica House,
London SW184LS
Nick Chapman

Atomic
0161 929 7221
www.atomicdesign.co.uk
Spooner House, 116A Ashley
Road, Hale Cheshire WA14 2UN
Lianne Ramsden

Atticmedia
020 7490 8789
www.atticmedia.com
34 Waterside, 44-48 Wharf Road,
Islington, London N1 7UX
Ross Baird

Avid Creative
01252 720806
www.avidcreative.co.uk
Old Chambers, 93-94 West Street,
Farnham, Surrey GU9 7EB
Mr Wallace

Avvio Design
01189 404444
www.avvio.co.uk
The Quadrant, Upper Culham
Farm, Cockpool Green,
Berkshire RG10 8NR
James Norrington /
Linda Johansson

Big Picture Interactive
01926 422002
www.bigpictureinteractive.co.uk
9 Parade, Leamington Spa,
Warwickshire CV32 4DG
Rebecca Dempsey

The names included are contacts for junior creative positions and work placements

Bite
020 7253 2500
www.anotherbiteidea.com
11 Northburgh Street,
London EC1V 0AH
Clare Rayburn

Bloom Design
020 7924 4533
www.bloom-design.com
25 The Village, 101 Arnies St.
London SW11 2JW
Dan Cornell / Polly Williams

Blue Marlin
01225 310444
www.bluemarlinbd.com
The Tram Sheds, Beehive Yard,
Walcot Street, Bath, BA1 5BD
Antonia Ecklsley /
Shelly Dyer-Gibbins

Bostock and Pollitt
020 7379 6709
www.bostockandpollitt.com
9-10 Floral Street,
London WC2E 9HW
Kevin Macey

Boxer
01675 467050
www.boxer.uk.com
St. Phillips Court, Churchill, Coles
Hill, Birmingham B46 3AD
Paul Cattledine / Jemma Narey

Brahm Design
01132 304000
www.brahm.com
The Brahm Building, Alma Road,
Headingley, Leeds LS6 2AH
Paul Nichols

Brandhouse WTS
020 7262 1707
www.brandhousewts.com
10a Frederick Close,
London W2 2HD
Mel Maynard / Keely Jackman

Brewer Riddiford
020 7240 9351
www.brewer-riddiford.co.uk
69 Shelton St, Covent Gdn,
London WC2H 9HE
John Wynne, Clare O'Brian and
Steve Booth

Browns
020 7407 9074
www.browns-design.co.uk
29 Queen Elizabeth Street,
London SE1 2LP
Chris Wilson / Rachel Veniard

C Eye
020 7490 2393
www.c-eye.co.uk
James House, 22-24
Corsham Street, London N1 6DR
Michael Sheridan

Carter Design Group
01858 433322
www.carterdesign.co.uk
North Lane, Foxton,
Leicestershire LE16 7RF
Steve Newitt / Derek Keyte

Carter Wong Tomlin
020 7569 0000
www.carterwongtomlin.com
29 Brook Mews, London W2 3BW
Phil Carter

Checkland Kindleysides
01162 644700
www.checkind.com
Charnwood Edge, Cossington,
Leicester LE7 4UZ
Judith Randall

CHP Design
020 7240 0466
www.chpdesign.com
76 Neal Street, Covent Garden,
London WC2H 9PA
Mark Hall

Christian Topf Design
01326 315551
www.ctd-studio.co.uk
65 Marlborouh Road, Falmouth,
Cornwall TR11 3LL
Christine Tops

Cimex Inc
020 7359 4664
www.cimex.com
53-55 Scrutton Street,
London EC2A 4XL

Az Mohammed
Circle Line
01245 473831/478550
www.circlelinedesign.co.uk
60 High Street, Great Baddow,
Chelmsford, Essex CM2 7HH
Rob Stone

Clear Design
0117 3770727
www.cleardesignuk.com
1 Gas Ferry Road,
Bristol BS1 6UN
Michael Hawkins

Coast Design
0117 923 9911
www.coast-design.com
10 Clifton Road, Clifton,
Bristol BS8 1AF
Greg Dash

Coley Porter Bell
020 7824 7700
www.cpb.co.uk
18 Grosvenor Gdns,
London SW1W 0DH
Nicky Triggs

Communiqué 360
020 8940 4444
www.communique-group.com
52 Worple Way, Richmond,
Surrey TW10 6DF
Greg McKenzie

Conchango
01784 222222
www.conchango.com
Heritage House, Church Road,
Egham, Surrey TW20 9QD
Charlotte Cook

Conran & Partners
020 7403 8899
www.conranandpartners.com
22 Shad Thames, London
SE1 2YU
Katy Clarke

Conran Design Group
020 7566 4566
www.conrandesigngroup.com
90-98 Goswell Road,
London EC1V 7DF
Sarah Taylor

Corporate Edge
020 7855 5888
www.corporateedge.com
149 Hammersmith Road,
London W14 0QL
Ruth Aspalla

Coutts Retail Communications
020 7510 9292
www.crc-uk.com
Violet Road, London E3 3QL
Carol Judge

CRA Design Ltd.
020 7269 8660
www.cra-design.co.uk
5 Great James Street,
London WC1N 3DB
Colin Robinson

Crab Creative
020 7700 1020
www.crabcreative.com
41 Hemingford Road,
London N1 1BY
Costas Mithalia

Craik Jones Digital
020 7734 1650
www.digital.craikjones.co.uk
120 Regent Street,
London W1B 5RY
Mark Buckingham

Creative Leap
020 7549 0700
www.creativeleap.com
Northburgh House, 10
Northburgh St, London EC1V0AT
Richard Haywood

Crescent Lodge
020 7613 0613
www.crescentlodge.co.uk
Foundation House, Perseverance
Works, London E2 8DD
David Lovelock

Dalziel and Pow
020 7837 7117
www.dalziel-pow.co.uk
5-8 Hardwick Street,
London EC1R 4RG
Rosalyn Scott

Delaney Design Consultants
01892 523427
www.delaneydesign.co.uk
42 Prospect Rd, Tunbridge Wells,
Kent TN2 4SH
Mr or Mrs Delaney

Design Bridge
020 7814 9922
www.designbridge.com
International Design Consultants,
18 Clerkenwell Close,
London EC1R 0QN
Kirsty Rafferty

Design House
01274 378848
www.thedesignhouse.com
Perkin House, 1 Longlands Street,
Bradford, West Yorkshire BD1 2TP
Darren Wake

Design UK
020 7292 2700
www.designuk.com
12-14 Denman Street, Piccadilly,
London W1D 7HJ
Christian Hoper

Designunity
020 7403 5535
www.designunity.co.uk
Andrew Beattie

Dew Gibbons
020 7689 8999
www.dewgibbons.com
49 Tabernacle Street,
London EC2A 4AA
Nikky Campbell

Din Associates
020 7582 0777
www.din.co.uk
32 St Oswald's Place,
London SE11 5JE
Wendy Hawker

DJPA
020 7470 6700
www.djpa.com
Unit I-4, 22-24 Torrington Place,
London WC1E 7HF

Alia Naqvi DLKW Dialogue
020 7836 3474
www.dlkwdialogue.com
25 Wellington Street,
London WC2E 7DA

DNA Consulting
020 7357 0573
www.dna.co.uk
1 Berners Street,
London W1T 3LA
Jo Marvell

Dow Carter
020 7689 1200
www.dowcarter.com
48 Rawstorne Street,
London EC1V 7ND
Kelvin Tillinghast

Dutton Merrifield
01173 179293
www.dutton-merrifield.co.uk
Langford Lodge, 109 Pembroke
Road, Clifton, Bristol BS8 3EX
Alison Green

DVA
01256 882032
www.dva.co.uk
7/8 Campbell Court, Bramley,
Tadley, Hampshire RG26 5EG
Barry Gibson

E3 Media
01179 021333
www.e3media.co.uk
2nd Floor, The Tobacco Factory,
Raleigh Road, Southville,
Bristol BS3 1TF
Wesley Hogg / Vicky James

Elmwood
01943 870229
www.elmwood.co.uk
Ghyll Royd, Guiseley,
Leeds LS20 9LT
John Stubley / Andrew Lawrence

Emperor Design Consultants
020 7729 9090
www.emperordesign.co.uk
Zetland House, 5/25 Scrutton
Street, London EC2A 4HJ
Neil Davies

Enterprise IG
020 8943 9555
www.ksdp.com
Burgoine Quay, 8 Lower
Teddington Road, Hampton
Wick, Surrey KT1 4ER
Jo Saker

Enterprise IG
020 7559 7000
www.enterpriseig.com
11-33 St John Street,
London EC1M 4PJ
Justin Reed / Laura Price-Bates

Felton Communication
020 7405 0900
www.felton.co.uk
2 Bleeding Heart Yard,
London EC1N 8SJ
Roger Felton

Finisterre
020 7357 9333
www.finisterre.co.uk
The Shiva Building,
The Tanneries, Bermondsey
Street, London SE1 3XH
Kate Gorringe

Firedog Design
020 7292 6270
www.firedog-design.co.uk
32 Lexington Street, Soho,
London W1F OLQ
Clifford Boobyer

Flame Design
020 7012 1671
www.flamedesign.co.uk
Studio 1.1, Hoxton Works,
128 Hoxton Street,
London N1 6SH
Emma Atkinson

FLB
01242 245851
www.flb.co.uk
De La Bere House, Bayshill Road,
Cheltenham GL50 3AW
Colin Mechan

Four IV Design Consultants
020 7837 8659
www.fouriv.com
Exmouth House, 3 Pine Street,
London EC1R OJH
Holly Budgen / Celine Leterme

FPP Design
0191 261 6662
www.fppdesign.com
The Court Yard, 1 Dinsdale Place,
Newcastle upon Tyne NE2 1BD
Carol Pettinger

Fraserdesign
01442 200400
www.fraserdesign.com
The Barns, London Road, Bourne
End, Hertfordshire HP1 2RH
Andrew Fraser

Frost Design
020 7490 7994
www.frostdesign.co.uk
The Gymnasium, Kings Way Place,
London EC1R OLU

Fuel Design
020 7377 2697
www.fuel-design.com
33 Fournier Street,
London E1 6QE
Damon Murray / Stephen Sorrell

Futurebrand
020 7556 9797
www.futurebrand.com
Fox Court, 14 Gray's Inn Road,
London WC1X 8WS
Ronnie Smith

GDA Design
01661 844777
www.gda-design.co.uk
Hindley Hall, Stocksfield,
Northumberland NE43 7RY
Edward Gainsford

Graphico New Media
01635 522810
www.graphico.co.uk
Goldwell House, Old Bath Road,
Newbury, Berks RG14 1JH
Andy Holden

Gyro Group
020 7351 1550
www.gyrocreative.com
603 The Chambers, Chelsea
Harbour, London SW10 OXF
Darren Bolton

Haygarth
020 8971 3300
www.haygarth.co.uk
Haygarth House, 28-31 High
Street , Wimbledon Village,
London SW19 5BY
Martin Steel / Philippa Johns /
Bob Blandford

Holmes and Marchant
01628 890890
www.hmi-huntsworth.com
Marlow Place, Station Road,
Marlow, Bucks, Sl7 1NB
Nick Hanson

Hunter Lodge Design
01923 714949
www.hunterlodge.co.uk
171 High Street, Rickmansworth,
Hertfordshire WD3 1AY
Mike Stonelake / Peter Walker /
Mark Chapman

IC Design
020 8748 2536
www.icdesign.co.uk
1 Galena Road, London W6 OLT
Alex Haddon

Idealogical
01525 221822
www.idealogical.co.uk
Beacon House, Orchard Farm,
Ivinghoe Aston LU7 9DL
Fiona Heap

Identikal
020 7253 6771
www.identikal.com
Nick Hayes / Adam Hayes

Imagination
020 7323 3300
www.imagination.com
25 Store Street, South Crescent,
London WC1E 7BL
Sally Crabb

Immaculate
020 8987 8900
www.immaculateuk.com
500 Chiswick High Road,
London W4 5RG
Phil Staff

Incepta Online
020 7282 2800
www.inceptaonline.com
3 London Wall Buildings,
London EC2M 5SY

Indent Design
0118 986 1672
www.indentdesign.co.uk
2 Denmark Road,
Reading RG1 5PA
Jo Dennis

Indigo
020 8858 5100
www.indigocreative.co.uk
49 Burney Street, Greenwich,
London SE10 8EX
John Roser

The names included are contacts for junior creative positions and work placements

Innocence
020 7554 1200
www.innocence.co.uk
85 Strand, London WC2R 0DW
Georgina Collins

Interbrand
020 7554 1000
www.interbrand.com
85 Strand, London WC2R 0DW
Andy Payne / Sian Penhallow

Interesource
020 7613 8200
www.interesource.co.uk
50-52 Paul Street,
London EC2A 4LB
Ian Howlett / Tim Malbon

Intro
020 7324 3244
www.intro-uk.com
42 St. John Street,
London EC1M 4DL
Jo Marsh

Jack Morton Inc
020 8735 2000
www.jackmorter.co.uk
16-18 Acton Park Estate,
Stanley Gardens, The Vale,
London W3 7QE
Fiona Lawlor

Jackson Bird
01543 415549
www.jacksonbird.co.uk
Three Spires House, Station Road,
Lichfield WS13 6HX
Adrian Jackson

johnson Banks
020 7587 6400
www.johnsonbanks.co.uk
Crescent Works, Crescent Lane,
Clapham, London SW4 9RW
Kath Tudball

Jones Knowles Ritchie
020 7428 8000
www.jkr.co.uk
128 Albert Street,
London NW1 7NE
Lou Smith

Jump Media
0117 929 4456
www.jumpmedia.co.uk
3 Church Road, Penryn,
Falmouth, Cornwall TR10 8DA
Nick Wylie

Kemistry
020 7729 3636
http://www.kemistry.co.uk
43 Charlotte Road, Shoreditch,
London EC2A 3PD
Graham McCullen

Kugel
020 7478 8300
www.kugel.co.uk
55 Greek St, London W1D 3DT
Phil Birchall / Kate Brooks

Lambie Nairn
020 7802 5800
www.lambie-nairn.com
Greencoat House,
15 Francis Street, London
SW1P 1DH
Gary Holt

Lateral
020 7613 4449
www.lateral.net
Charlotte House, 47-49 Charlotte
Road, London EC2A 3QT
Su Sareen / Colin Douglas

Lighthouse
01224 627396
www.lighthouse-graphics.co.uk
Belgrave House, Belgrave
Terrace, Aberdeen AB25 2NR
John Duncan

Lightmaker
0161 834 9889
www.lightmaker.com
Century Place,
Buildings 3 & 4, Lamberts Road,
Tunbridge Wells TN2 3EH
Joe Saunders

Lime Lizard
01676 525173
www.limelizard.co.uk
Meriden Hall, Main Road,
Meriden, CV7 7PT
Richard Hickman

Linney Design
01623 450460
www.linneydesign.com
Adamsway, Mansfield, NG18 4FL
Andy Rogers

Lloyd Ferguson Hawkins BIC
020 7706 8762
www.lfh.co.uk
6a-10 Frederick Close, Stanhope
Place, London W2 2HD

LMC
020 7727 7344
www.lmcdesign.co.uk
The Walmer Courtyard, 225-227
Walmer Rd, London W11 4EY
David Johnston

Magnetic North
0161 228 7171
www.magneticn.co.uk
Canada House, Chepstow Street,
Manchester, M1 5FW
Janet Harrison

Malone Design
020 7323 2232
www.malonedesign.co.uk
104 Great Portland,
London W1W 6PE

Mansfields
01268 520646
www.mansfieldsdesign.co.uk
Bentails, Pipps Hill Industrial
Estate, Basildon, Essex SS14 3BX
Grant Harris

Marketplace Design
01235 554499
www.marketplace-design.co.uk
Pulpit House, 1 The Sq.,
Abingdon, Oxfordshire OX14 5SZ
Colin Goodall / Mike Gilling

Met Studio Design
020 7378 7348
www.metstudio.com
5 Maidstone Building Mews,
72-76 Borough High Street,
London SE1 1GN
Jo Muncaster / Alex McCuig

Metaphor
020 7449 2949
www.mphor.co.uk
47 St. Johns Wood High Street,
St. Johns Wood, NW8 7NJ
Stephen Greenberg

Micrographix
01869 250806
www.micrographix.co.uk
Unit A3, Rowood Estate, Murdock
Road, Bicester, OX26 4PP
Mike Linzey

Millini
020 8974 3333
www.millini.co.uk
81 Barwel Business Park,
Chessington, Surrey KT9 2NY
Tony Sharman

**Minale Tattersfield Design
Strategy**
020 8948 7999
www.mintat.co.uk
The Poppy Factory, 20 Petersham
Road, Richmond TW10 6UR
Alex Maranzano

Minima Design
01728 727000
www.minima.co.uk
The Technology Centre,
Framlingham, Suffolk IP13 9EZ
Matt Horsup

MO Design
01550 740150
www.mo-design.com
Glynhir, Llanddeusant,
Llangagog SA19 9AJ
Rebecca Ingleby

MPC Creative
0161 236 4646
www.mpccreative.com
75 Lever Street, The Northern
Quarter, Manchester M1 1FL
Ted Holden

Natural Associates
020 7490 4575
www.naturalassociates.com
55 Charterhouse Street,
London EC1M 6HA
Linda Vaux

Navyblue Design
020 7253 0316
www.navyblue.com
Third Floor Morelands,
5-23 Old Street, London EC1V 9HL
Clare Lundy

NE6 Design Consultants
0191 221 2606
www.ne6design.co.uk
4 St. James Terrace,
Newcastle upon Tyne NE1 4NE
Chris Lumley

New Media Designs
01484 404 460
www.newmediadesigns.co.uk
106 Commercial Street,
Brighouse,
West Yorkshire HD6 1AQ
Mark Rushworth

Nim Design
020 8426 6888
www.nimdesign.com
The Old Bank, 92 High Street,
Harrow on the Hill,
Middlesex HA1 3LP
Sue Crossing

North Star Design
01282 865333
www.northstardesign.co.uk
Suite 1, The Exchange,
Spring Lane, Colne BB8 9BD
Chris Lamle

Nucleus
020 8398 9133
www.nucleus.co.uk
John Loftus House,
Summer Road, Thames Ditton,
Surrey KT7 0RD
Suzanne Lykiard

Oakley Wilkinson Bryan
0121 250 3568
www.owb.uk.com
Faraday Wharf, Holt Street,
Aston Science Park
Birmingham B7 4BB
Andy Wilkinson

Oakwood Design Consultants
01179 836789
www.oakwood-dc.com
7 Park Street, Bristol BS1 5NF
Tony Marwick

ocean70
0141 221 2337
www.ocean70.com
Pentagon Centre,
36 Washington Street,
Glasgow, G3 8AZ
Alex Stewart

Origin Design
01494 722211
www.origindesign.biz
1 Church Street, Old Amersham,
Bucks., HP7 0DB
Graeme Collins

OTM
020 7478 4400
www.otmbrand.com
12 Goslett Yard,
London WC2H 0EQ
Sharon Luckett

Outside Line
020 7636 5511
www.outsideline.co.uk
Butler House, 177-178 Tottenham
Court Road, London
Lloyd Falmons

Out-Think
0113 285 6500
www.out-think.com
Rose Wharf, East Street,
Leeds LS9 8EE
David Bell

Oyster Partners
020 7446 7500
www.oyster.com
1 Naoroji Street, off Margery
Street, London WC1X 0JD
Clare Myerson

Panic Design
01256 895438
www.panicdesign.co.uk
12B Laverstoke Lane,
Laverstoke, Whitchurch,
Hampshire RG28 7NY
Alice Bloor

Parker Williams Design
020 8995 6411
www.parkerwilliamsdesign.co.uk
1st Floor, Boysey House, Barley
Mow Passage, London W4 4PT
Shireen Painter

Paul Martin Design Company
01730 265814
www.pmdc.co.uk
32 Dragon Street, Petersfield,
Hampshire GU31 4JJ
Paul Martin

PDD
020 8735 1111
www.pdd.co.uk
85-87 Richford Street,
London W6 7HJ
Fay Bradley

PDG GRAPHICS
0115 967 8555
www.pdggraphics.com
Media House, Padge Road,
Nottingham NG9 2RS
Russ Tomlin

Pearlfisher
020 7603 8666
www.pearlfisher.com
50 Brook Green, Hammersmith,
London W6 7BJ
Emma Turbutt

Pebble Graphics
01794 523811
www.pebblegraphics.co.uk
The Studio, Church Place,
Romsey, Hampshire SO51 8NG
Nick Johnson

Pedalo
0845 644 2668
www.pedalo.co.uk
Power Road Studios, 114 Power
Road, London W4 5PY Tom Porter

Pemberton & Whitefoord
020 7723 8899
www.p-and-w.com
Ivor House, 21 Ivor Place,
Marylebone, London NW1 6EU
Lee Newham

Pentagram Design Ltd
020 7229 3477
www.pentagram.co.uk
11 Needham Road,
London W11 2RP
Johanna Mohs

Pexton Searle
07000 355200
www.pextonsearle.co.uk
Oak Yard, Queens's Road,
Watford, Hertfordshire WD17 2QL
Peter Cronin

Peyton @ The Place
0870 420 2414
www.peyton-theplace.com
2 Sheraton Street,
London W1F 8BH
Peyton Martin

Pierrot Print and Design
01483 899000
www.pierrot.uk.com
Birtley Courtyard, Birtley Road,
Bramley, Guildford,
Surrey GU5 0LA
Monique Bure

Plus One Design
0117 9238638
www.plus-one.co.uk
10 Apsley Road, Clifton,
Bristol BS8 2SP
Ray Fussell

Pluspurple
01727 832487
www.pluspurple.com
Jubille House, 6 Cavendish Road,
St. Albans AL1 5EE
Bernd Wuthrich

Pocknell Studio
01787 463206
www.pocknellstudio.com
Pocknell, Readings, Blackmore
End, Braintree, Essex CM7 4DH
Fern Hammerton

Point Blank Inc.
020 7291 8320
www.pointblankinc.co.uk
16 Gresse Street, London W1T 1QL
David Uprichard

Poke
020 7749 5353
www.pokelondon.com
Biscuit Building,
10 Redchurch Street,
London E2 7DD

Pop Creative
07799 631981
www.popcreative.co.uk
13 Church Street, Oswestry,
Shropshire SY11 2SU

Poulter Partners
0113 2856500
www.poultergroup.com
Rose Wharf, East Street,
Leeds LS9 8EE
Sally Gaunt / Corinne Pujara

Practise
020 74503 3175
www.practise.co.uk
18-24 Shacklewell Lane,
London E8 2EZ

Precedent Communications
020 7216 1300
www.precedent.co.uk
109-123 Clifton Street,
London EC2A 4LD
Beverley Sullivan

Preloaded
020 7684 3505
www.preloaded.com
16-24 Underwood Street,
London N1 7JQ
Phil Stewart

Progressive Edge
0845 257 6071
www.progressive-edge.co.uk
5 Bold Place, Liverpool L1 9DN

Project 1 Design
01865 204417
www.p1d.co.uk
225 Cowley Road,
Oxford OX4 1XG
Phil Robson

Pure Design
0131 220 5522
www.puredesign.co.uk
8 Randolph Crescent,
Edinburgh, EH3 7TH
Matthew Weaver

Purple Circle
01159 550005
www.purplecircle.co.uk
Global Headquarters, 1 Howard
Street, Nottingham NG1 3LT
Darren Fisk

Q Box Ltd.
0116 24 24 051
www.qbox.co.uk
14 Saffron Road, Wigston,
Leicester LE18 4TD

Questar Comms
01709 371100
www.questar.co.uk
Linden House, 34 Moorgate Road,
Rotherham S60 2AG
Lynne Dawson

Radley Yeldar
020 7033 0700
www.ry.com
24 Charlotte Road,
London EC2A 3PB

The names included are contacts for junior creative positions and work placements

Raincoat
01761 233 200
www.raincoat.co.uk
The Granary, Manor Courtyard,
Stratton on the Fosse,
Bath BA3 4QF
Nick Kenyon

Random Media
020 7684 4848
www.randommedia.co.uk
10-18 Vestry Street,
London N1 7RE
Mark Griffiths

Ratcliffe Fowler Design
01162 420200
www.ratcliffefowlerdesign.co.uk
2 Chancery Place, Milstone Lane,
Leicester LE1 5JN
Matt Tomlin / Mike Ratcliffe

Reading Room
020 7025 1800
www.readingroom.com
53 Frith St, Soho,
London W1D 4SN
Margaret Manning /
Simon Usher

Realise
020 7743 7150
www.realise.com
148 Leadenhall Street,
London EC3V 4QT
Matthew Powell / Tony Murphy

Recollective
020 7064 4196
www.recollective.co.uk
Studio 2, Alaska Building 600,
61 Grange Road, London SE1 3BB
Francis O'Reilly

Red Flare Ltd.
01789 450780
www.redflare.co.uk
Granary House, Tythe Barn
Court, Alderminster,
Warwickshire CV37 8NX

Red Rocket
01392 824322
www.redrocket.uk.com
6A Cranmere Court, Matford
Business Park, Exeter EX2 8PW
Gary Martin / Jane Mason

**Redhouse Lane
Communications**
020 7462 2600
www.redhouselane.co.uk
14-15 Bedford Square,
London WC1B 3JA

Redpath
0131 556 9115
www.redpath.co.uk
5 Gayfield Square,
Edinburgh EH1 3NW
Andrew Hunter / Ian Lauder

Redstone
0845 200 2200
www.redstone.co.uk
80 great Eastern Street,
London EC2A 3RS
Kate O'Connell

**Refinery Marketing
Communications**
0161 273 5511
www.refinerygroup.co.uk
10 Pitbrook Street,
Manchester M12 6JX
David Pye

Reflex Digital
0113 200 7017
www.reflex.net
Host Media Centre, 21 Savile
Mount, Leeds LS7 3HZ

Roar
01564 796200
www.roarcreativity.co.uk
123 High Street, Henley in Arden,
Warwickshire B95 5AU
Kevin Roberts

Room for Design
01609 777554
www.roomfordesign.co.uk
Register House, Northallerton,
North Yorkshire DL6 1NB
Joe Essex

Rufus Leonard
020 7404 4490
www.rufusleonard.com
The Drill Hall, 57a Farringdon
Road, London EC1M 3JB
Andrew Fleming / Steve Howell /
Lucy Kay

Salivate
01276 504629
www.slv8.com
Rockley House, 14 Meadway,
Camberley, Surrey GU16 8TQ
Tina Smith

Sammakko Design
07779 275287
www.sammakko.co.uk
193 St. James Road, Croydon,
Surrey CRO 2BZ

SAS
020 7243 3232
www.sasdesign.co.uk
6 Salem Road, London W2 4BU
Gilmar Wendt

Sauce Design
020 7813 2098
www.saucedesign.co.uk
57 Farringdon Road,
London EC1M 3JB
Dan Rolfe

Scarlett
01908 516444
www.scarlettdesign.co.uk
Glebe House, Glebe
Lane, Hanslope,
Buckinghamshire, MK19 7DD

Sedgwick Richardson
020 7404 7913
www.sedgwick-richardson.com
3rd Floor, 26 Gray's Inn Road,
London WC1X 8HR
Duncan Tynner

Sedley Place
020 7627 5777
www.sedley-place.co.uk
68 Venn Street, London SW4 0AX
Fiona Nash

Sequence
0845 100 400
www.sequence.co.uk
Fitzalan House, Fitzalan Road,
Cardiff CF24 OEL

Seymour Powell
020 7381 6433
www.seymourpowell.com
327 Lillie Road, London SW6 7NR
Maria Fredrickson

Shaw Design Associates
020 7265 8826
www.shaw-design.co.uk
Rutland House, 42-46 New Road,
London E1 2AX
Matt Shaw

Shelfstacker
07782 273544
www.shelfstackerltd.com
15 Abercorn Way,
London SE1 5HL

Shelton Fleming Associates
020 7351 2420
www.sheltonfleming.co.uk
35 Chelsea Wharf, Lots Road,
London SW10 0QJ
Emma Wynne

Sheppard Day Associates
020 7821 2222
www.sheppard-day.com
The Friary, 47 Francis Street,
London SW1P 1QR
Tracey Barr

SHH
020 8600 4171
www.shh.co.uk
1 Vencourt Place, Ravenscourt
Park, Hammersmith,
London W6 9NU
Graham Harris

Siebert Head
020 7689 9090
www.sieberthead.com
80 Goswell Road,
London EC1V 7DB
Rhoda Maw

Sigma Engineering Product
Design Ltd
01563 539 007
www.sigmaepd.com
Unit 5, Block 5, Moorfield
Industrial Estate,
Kilmarnock KA2 OAG
Ross Dobbie

Silver Chair
01442 400612
www.silverchair.co.uk
27 Queensway, Old Town, Hemel
Hempstead, Herts HP1 1LS
Niccola Tadelhauser

Simon Morris Associates
01689 604221
www.smadesign.org.uk
Ravensquay, Orpington BR5 4BQ
Tamara De Schetter /
Simon Morris

Sinclair Media
01604 879234
www.sinclairmedia.net
21 Station Road, Blisworth,
Northants NN7 3DS
Donald Turnbull

Sirocco Design
07742 538364
www.siroccodesign.co.uk
6 Newbury Place, Warsash,
Hampshire SO31 9TH

Size Creative
020 7239 1300
www.sizecreative.com 58-62
White Lion Street,
London N1 9PP
Deborah Hall / Richard Jenner

Sliwa Creative
0845 226 0995
www.sliwacreative.com
66 Lower Street, Stansted
Mountfichet, Essex CM24 8LR

Small Back Room
020 7701 4227
www.smallbackroom.com
88 Camberwell Road,
London SE5 OEG
Chi-Man Tsang

Smartstudiosuk
01782 377434
www.smartstudiosuk.com
The Sutherland Institute,
Lightwood Road, Longton,
Stoke on Trent ST3 4HY
Ian Hammersley

Smith & Milton
020 7608 4242
www.smith-milton.co.uk
The Hot House, 44-46 Sekford
Street, London EC1R OHA
Craig Burrows

Smith Design
0797 697 7281
www.smithltd.co.uk
The Studio 2B, Cockburn Street,
Cambridge CB1 3NB

Smoketank
0870 991 5010
www.smoketank.com
46 Maddox Street,
London W15 1QA
Nick Rose

Smooth Design
01296 393977
www.smoothdesign.com
63 Buckingham Street, Aylesbury,
Bucks HP20 2NF
Chris Underwood

So Creative
020 7247 4863
www.so-creative.com
The Old Truman Brewery,
91 Brick Lane, London E1 6QL
Lisa Oliver

Spin
020 7793 9555
www.spin.co.uk
12 Canterbury Court, Kennington
Park, 1/3 Brixton Road,
London SW9 6DE
Tony Brook

Splashdown
020 8222 6612
www.splashdown.co.uk
Unit 2D + 2C Westpoint, 36-37
Warple Way, London W3 0RG
Mark Pritchard

Splendid
020 7287 4442
www.howsplendid.com
54-62 Regent Street,
London W1B 5RE
Paul Bishop

Splinter
0151 709 9066
www.splinter.co.uk
2nd Floor, Baird House,
Edge Lane, Liverpool L7 9NJ
Rachael Boden

Spread Design
020 7241 2991
www.spread-design.co.uk
35 Charlotte Road,
London EC2A 3PB
Stuart Taylor

Spring Digital
0845 009 6790
www.springdigital.co.uk
13 Church Street,
London NW8 8DT

Springer Jacoby Design
020 7880 4700
www.sj.com
159-173 St John Street,
London EC1V 4RS
Jan Lorenz

Springetts Design Consultants
020 7486 7527
www.springetts.co.uk 13
Salisbury Place, London W1H 1FJ
Victoria Newman

Spud Design
01527 579 980
www.spud-design.co.uk
76 Millfield Road,
Bromsgrove B61 7BL

Spyre Ltd.
07932 062060
www.spyre.ltd.uk
29 Tithe Court, Lanley,
Berkshire SL3 8AS

St Cross Design Communications
01707 260044
www.st-x.co.uk
87 Great North Road,
Hatfield, Herts AL9 5DA
Jason Gale

Start Creative
020 7269 0101
www.startcreative.co.uk
2 Sheraton Street, Soho,
London W1F 8BH
Mark Smith and Martin Muir

Staunch Design
01423 567707
www.staunch.com

Steel Design
020 8871 2656
www.steel-design.co.uk
521-525 Old York Road,
Wandsworth, London SW18 1TG
Nick Bennett / Amanda Wheeler

Stevenson Sharpe
0141 341 4100
www.stevensonsharpe.co.uk
44 Spiers Wharf,
Glasgow G4 9TH

Stills Design
029 2035 3940
www.stillsdesign.com
The Old Church, 76 Wells Street,
Canton, Cardiff CF11 6DY
Chris Carpenter

Stocks Taylor Benson
01162 387833
www.stbdesign.co.uk
The Forge, Narborough Wood
Park, Desford Road, Enderby,
Leicestershire LE19 4XT
Darren Seymour

Stone Soup
01904 673767
www.stone-soup.co.uk
9-11 Barleycorn Yard,
Walmgate, York YO1 9TX
Tom Sharp

Studio 401
01935 813176
www.studio401.co.uk
2 Coldharbour Business Park,
Sherborne, Dorset DT9 4JW
Mark Holgate

Studio North Ltd.
0161 237 5151
www.studionorth.co.uk
Waulk Mill, 51 Bengal Street,
Manchester M4 6LN
Nick Wright

Stylo Design
020 8964 9273
www.stylodesign.co.uk
Bedford Chambers, The Piazza,
Covent Garden,
London WC2E 8HA

Sumo Design
0191 261 9894
www.sumodesign.co.uk
71 Westgate Road,
Newcastle upon Tyne,
Tyne and Wear NE1 1SG
Jim Richardson

Sussed Design
01273 275302
www.susseddesign.com
1st Floor, 106 Coleridge Street,
Hove, East Sussex BN3 5AA

Swamp
0845 1202405
www.swampme.com
103 Clarendon Road,
Leeds LS2 9DF
Andrew Brown

Synapse Creative Ltd.
01923 239444
www.synapse-creative.com
18 Paramount Industrial
Estate, Sandown Road,
Watford WD24 7XG
Richard Walker

Syzygy
020 7460 4080
www.syzygy.net
4th Floor, Elsley House,
24-30 Great Titchfield Street,
London W1W 8BF
Rachel Stretch / Kate Riley

Take Aim
0117 3307546
www.takeaimdesign.co.uk
Royal Colonnades, 16 Great
George Street, Bristol BS1 5RH
Mike Jenkins

Tatham Design
020 8932 2851
www.tathamdesign.co.uk
11 Keith Grove, London W12 9EY
Amanda Tatham

Tayburn
0131 662 0662
www.tayburn.co.uk
15 Kittle Yards, Causewayside,
Edinburgh EH9 1PJ
Catherine Gillon

TBG Ltd.
020 7428 6650
www.tbgltd.com
100 Highgate Studios, 53-79
Highgate Road, London NW5 1TL
Chris Ball

TGV Design & Marketing
020 8852 9448
www.tgvdesign.co.uk
St Agnes House, Cresswell Park,
Blackheath, London SE3 9RJ
Colin Beckenham

The Brewery
020 8439 8400
www.thebrewery-london.com
18 Petersham Road, Richmond,
London TW10 6UW
Katie Davies / Paul Stead

The Chase (London)
020 7927 0821
www.thechase.co.uk
22 Newman St. London W1T 1PH
Steve Royle

The names included are contacts for junior creative positions and work placements

The Chase (Manchester)
0161 832 5575
www.thechase.co.uk
1 North Parade, Parsonage
Gardens, Manchester M3 2NH
Alan Herron

The Church Agency
01234 404040
www.thechurchagency.com
6 Franklin Court, Stannard Way,
Priory Business Park,
Bedford MK44 3JZ
Sarah Chiazza

The Conservatory
020 7278 3222
www.theconservatory.co.uk
210 Spitfire Studios, 63-71 Collier
Street, London N1 9BE
Andy Green

The Creative Store
020 8543 3855
www.thecreativestore.co.uk
142 Merton Hall Road,
Wimbledon, London SW19 3PZ
Serena Price

The Design Conspiracy
020 7470 8841
www.thedesignconspiracy.com
11-15 Betterton Street, London
WC2H 9BP
Ben Terrett

The Design Group
020 7608 1144
www.the-design-group.co.uk
111 Charterhouse Street,
London EC1M 6AW
Valeria Correa

The Formation
020 7739 8198
www.theformation-cc.co.uk
59 Charlotte Road,
London EC2A 3QW
Adrian Kilby

The Forster Company
020 7403 2230
www.forstercreative.co.uk
49 Southwark Street,
London SE1 1RU
Andrew Pate

The Group
020 7436 3140
www.the-group.net
PO BOX 4387, 6-10 Great Portland
Street, London W1A 7SP
Jenny Bent

The Hamiltons
020 7407 9501
www.thehamiltons.co.uk
8 The Glasshouse, 3 Royal Oak
Yard, London SE1 3GE
Clare Hamilton

The Hub
020 8560 9222
www.thehub.co.uk
The Power House, 1 Linkfield
Road, Isleworth,
Middlesex TW7 6QG

The Nest
020 7689 8344
www.thenest.co.uk
20 Flaxman Terrace,
London WC1H 9AT
Haleema Mahmood

The Open Agency
020 7740 7000
www.openagency.com
Mill House, 8 Mill Street,
London SE1 2BA
Emma Bacon

The Tangent
01428 707844
www.thetangent.net
1 Lilac College, Northchapel,
West Sussex GU28 9HL
David Kerfloot

The Three Creative
0207 729 4864
www.thethreecreative.com
The Studio, 13 Gibraltar Walk,
Shoreditch, London E2 7LH

The Well
01924 266133
www.welldesigned.uk.com
Studio 5B, Horbury Business
Complex, Manor Road,
Horbury, Wakefield,
West Yorkshire WF4 6HH

Them London
020 8392 6868
www.themlondon.com
107 Mortlake High Street,
London SW14 8HQ
Francois Reynier

Think Farm
020 7439 4399
www.thinkfarm.co.uk
3rd Floor, 89-91 Wardour Street,
London W1F 0UB
Mark Norton

Third Eye Design
0141 332 3335
www.thirdeyedesign.co.uk
23 Newton Place, Glasgow,
Scotland G3 7PY
Kenny Allan

This Is Real Art
020 7253 2181
www.thisisrealart.com
17C Clerkenwell Road,
London EC1M 5RD
Georgina Lee

Thomas.Matthews
020 7403 4281
www.thomasmatthews.com
8 Disney Street,
London SE1 1JF
Chris Saltonstall

Thought
0191 269 3420
www.thought.co.uk
15 High Bridge, 1st Floor,
Newcastle upon Tyne NE1 1EW
Ben Anderson

Thought Bubble
020 7387 8890
www.thoughtbubble.com
58/60 Fitzroy Street,
London W1T 5BU

TMG
020 7261 1777
www.tmg.co.uk
36 Southwark Bridge Road,
London SE1 9EU

Toast
01295 266644
www.toastdesign.co.uk
15 South Bar, Banbury OX16 9AA
David Foreman

Tonic
020 7033 2888
www.tonic.co.uk
143 Shoreditch High Street,
London E1 6JE

Toothbone
020 8974 6058
www.toothbone.co.uk
76 Canbury Avenue, Kingston-
upon-Thames, Surrey KT2 6JR
Scott Blatchley

Tor Design
01706 231017
www.tordesign.co.uk
5 Ashen Bottom Cottages,
Rossendale, Lancashire BB4 6JY

Tudor Rose
0116 222 9900
www.tudor-rose.co.uk
Tudor House, 6 Friar Lane,
Leicester LE1 5RA
Leigh Trowbridge

Turnbull Ripley
020 7221 0110
www.turnbullripley.co.uk
Monmouth House, 87-93
Westbourne Grove,
London W2 4UL
Trebe Ripley

Turner Duckworth
020 8894 7190
www.turnerduckworth.com
Voysey House, Barley Mow
Passage, London W4 4PH
Christian Eager

Turquoise
020 7420 9900
www.turquoisebranding.com
16 Neal's Yard, Covent Garden,
London WC2H 9DP
Scott Manning

**Two Hundred By 200 Graphic
Design Studio**
01383 432608
www.twohundredby200.co.uk
RMPR Offices, 27 (Basement)
Canmore Street,
Dunfermline KY12 7NU
Sean Makin

Tynan D'Arcy
01753 833550
www.tynan-darcy.com
Alexandra Court, St Leonards
Road, Windsor SL4 3BP
Ian D'Arcy

Unit 9
020 7613 3330
www.unit9.com
43-44 Hoxton Square,
London N1 6PB
Piero Frescabaldi

Unreal
020 7379 8752
www.unreal-uk.com
12 Dyott Street,
London WC1A 1DE
Brian Eagle

Venture Three
020 7290 1950
www.venturethree.com
5D Shepher Street,
London W1J 7HP
Amanda Brewster / Paul
Townsend / Graham Jones

Vhd Creative Energy
0117 908 6666
www.vhd.co.uk
36 Queen Square,
Bristol BS1 4QS
Keith Hollister

Vibrandt
01753 624 242
www.vibrandt.co.uk
The Sandom Group, Old Brewery,
Russell Street, Windsor SL4 1HQ
Greg Vallance

Vision
01273 766300
www.visiondesign.co.uk
120 Queens Road,
Brighton BN1 3WB
Jason Bannister

Visual Eyes
020 7613 1777
www.visual-eyes-media.co.uk
117-121 Curtain Road,
London EC2A 3AD
Anthony Lester

Visual Format
0870 765 82 62
www.visual-format.net
Studio 50, Grover Court, Loampit
Hill, London SE13 7ST
Anna Sorreineino

Vivado
01245 256464
www.vivado.co.uk
43 Parkinson Drive,
Chelmsford, Essex CM1 3GU
Stephen Elefsen

Vivid Creative Consultants
0114 267 1144
www.vividcreative.com
392 Psalter Lane,
Sheffield S11 8UW
Stephen Aracri

VO Corporation
020 7938 3100
www.vo-corporation.com
1st Floor, 187 Kensington High
Street, London W8 6SH
Matt Gardener

Walker Izard
020 7893 7883
www.walkerizard.co.uk
Studio 13, St. Julians,
Sevenoaks TN15 ORX
Paul Izard

Wall Creative
020 7251 2004
www.wallcreative.com
42 Kingsway Place, Sans Walk,
London EC1R OUL
Sheridan Wall

Ware Anthony Rust
01223 566212
www.war.uk.com
Newnham Mill, Newnham Road,
Cambridge CB3 9EY
Richard Bland

Warm Red Design
020 8325 1117
www.warmred.com
The Old House, 36 Southend
Road, Beckenham, Kent BR3 5AR

Warwick Dipple Design
01788 535105
www.wddesign.co.uk
First Floor, No. 6 Somers Road,
Rugby, Warwickshire CV22 7DE
Warwick Dipple

WDPA Communications
020 7323 2480
www.wdpa.co.uk
First Floor, 151 Shaftesbury
Avenue, London WC2H 8AL

Wheel
020 7348 1000
www.wheel.co.uk
Beaumont House, Kensington
Village, Avonmore Road,
London W14 8TS
Dasa Malikova

White Room Studios
01926 888721
www.whiteroomuk.com
Cottage Farm Barn,
Old Milverton,
Leamington Spa CV32 6SA
John Weatherall

William Hall
020 7336 0003
www.williamhall.co.uk
Unit 39, Cornwell House,
21 Clerkenwell Green.
London EC1R ODX

Winkreative
020 7758 2700
www.winkreative.com
8 Grafton Street,
London W1S 4EL
Richard Spencer-Powel

Wolff Olins
020 7713 7733
www.wolff-olins.com
10 Regents Wharf,
All Saints Street, London N1 9RL
Lisa MacDonald

WPA Pinfold
020 7436 9219
www.wpa-pinfold.co.uk
Ex Libris, Nineveh Road,
Leeds LS11 9QG
Shane Tattersoll

Wren Rowe
020 7828 5333
www.wrenrowe.co.uk
4 Denbigh Mews,
London SW1V 2HQ
Paul Foulkes

XM London
020 7724 7228
www.xmlondon.com
121-141 Westboune terrace,
London W2 6JR

Yeah Communications
0117 954 4657
www.yeahcomms.co.uk
16-18 Whiteladies Road,
Clifton, Bristol BS8 2LG

Zard Creative
020 7608 0338
www.zardcreative.com
32-36 Aylesbury Street,
London EC1R OET
Mick Stacey / Terry Rendall

Zavial Design
01460 249434
www.zavial.com
Southlea Farm, Wigborough,
South Petherton,
Somerset TA13 5LP

Ziggurat
020 7969 7777
www.zigguratbrands.com
8-14 Vine Hill, Clerkenwell,
London EC1R 5DX
Alison Miguel

Zip Design
020 7372 4474
www.zipdesign.co.uk
Unit 2A, Queens Studios,
121 Salusbury Road,
London NW6 6RG
Mary Crowley

Zynk Design Consultants
0207 721 7444
www.zynkdesign.com
11 The Chandlery,
50 Westminster Bridge Road,
London SE1 7QY
Stavros Theodoulou

The names included are contacts for junior creative positions and work placements

advertising

1576 Advertising
0131 473 1576
www.1576.co.uk
25 Rutland Square,
Edinburgh EH1 2BW
Adrian Jeffery / Ruth Lees

23red
0870 0130023
www.23red.com
2nd Floor Elsley Court,
20-22 Great Titchfield Street,
London W1W 8BE
Lucy Carlson / Philippa Dunning

A V Browne Advertising
028 9032 0663
www.avb.co.uk
46 Bedford Street, Belfast,
Northern Ireland BT2 7GH
Mike Fleming / Stephen Moore

A Vision (London)
020 7287 9898
www.avisionlondon.co.uk
The Blue Building, 7-11 Lexington
Street, London W1F 9AF
Lydia Barklem

Abbott Mead Vickers.BBDO
020 7616 3500
www.amvbbdo.com
151 Marylebone Road,
London NW1 5QE
Emma Clark / Peter Souter /
Paul Brazier

Aerodeon
020 7629 0089
www.aerodeon.com
449 Oxford Street,
London W1L 2PS
Chris Bourke

Alcazar Limited
0191 224 4000
www.alcazar.co.uk
Old Maling Pottery, Walker Road,
Newcastle upon Tyne NE6 1AB
Hugh Cheswright

Anderson Lambert
01582 754000
www.andersonlambert.com
2 Kensworth Gate, High Street,
South Dunstable, Beds LU6 3HS
Paul Mcnally

Anderson Spratt Group
02890 802000
www.andersonspratt.com
Anderson House, 409 Holywood
Road, Belfast BT4 2GU
Philip Milnes

Arc Marketing
020 7751 1662
www.arcmarketing.com
Warwick Building, Kensington
Village, Avonmore Road,
London W14 8HQ
Simon Barwell Taylor

Archibald Ingall Stretton
020 7467 6100
www.aislondon.com
Berners House, 47-48 Berners
Street, London W1T 3NF
Anna Barker

**Ardmore Advertising &
Marketing**
028 9042 5344
www.ardmore.co.uk
Pavillions Office Park, Kinnegar
Drive, Holywood,
County Down BT18 9JQ
Larry McGarry / Paul Bowen

Artavia
01271 323333
www.artavia.co.uk
Artavia House, Queen Street,
Barnstable, Devon EX32 8HW
Mark Berridge

Atlas Advertising
020 7467 3140
www.atlasadvertising.co.uk
10 Welbeck Street,
London W1G 9YA
Dominick Lynch-Robinson

Barkers Scotland
0141 248 5030
www.barkersscotland.co.uk
234 West George Street,
Glasgow G2 4QY
Kenny Risk

Barrett Cernis
020 7663 3575
www.barrett.cernis.co.uk
77 Long Acre, London WC2E 9LB
Ray Barret

Barrett Howe Group
01753 869455
www.barretthowe.com
1 Curfew Yard, Thames Street,
Windsor, Berkshire SL4 1SN
Paul Aston

**Barrington Johnson Lorains &
Partners**
0161 831 7141
www.bjl.co.uk
Sunlight House, Quay Street,
Manchester M3 3JZ
Margaret Leigh / Ray Barrett

Bartle Bogle Hegarty
020 7734 1677
www.bbh.co.uk
60 Kingly Street, London W1B 5DS
John O'Keeffe / Matt Waller

Base 01
020 8943 9999
www.base01.co.uk
10-12 The Causeway, Teddington,
Middlesex TW11 0HE
David Thomas

BDH TBWA
0161 908 8600
www.bdhtbwa.co.uk
St Paul's, 781 Wilmslow Road,
Didsbury Village, Manchester,
Lancashire M20 2RW
Danny Brook-Taylor

Beatwax
020 7734 1965
www.beatwax.com
91 Berwick Street,
London W1F 0NE
Nick Roper

Big Picture Interactive
01926 422002
www.bigpictureinteractive.co.uk
9 Parade, Leamington Spa,
Warwickshire CV32 4DG
Becky Dempsey

Blair Fowles Advertising
01202 558111
www.blairfowles.co.uk
22 St Peters Road,
Bournemouth BH1 2LE
Colin Gibson

Bond Advertising
0131 476 8053
www.bondadvertising.com
47 Timber Bush,
Edinburgh EH6 6QH
Caroline Garrad

Boy Meets Girl S&J
020 7012 6000
www.boymeetsgirl.sj.com
Fourth Floor, 159-173 St John
Street, London EC1V 4RS
Kate Stanners

Burkitt DDB
020 7320 9300
www.burkittddb.com
1 East Poultry Avenue,
London EC1A 9PT
Kirsty Petrie

Byron Advertising
01895 252131
www.thebyrongroup.com
Byron House, Wallingford Road,
Uxbridge, Middlesex UB8 2RW
Matthew Allen /
Daniel Billingham

Campbell Doyle Dye
020 7483 9800
www.cddlondon.com
4 Utopia Village, Chalcot Road,
London NW1 8LH
Laura Green-Wilkinson

**Charterhouse Advertising &
Marketing**
0161 848 9050
www.charterhouse-
advertising.co.uk
West Point, 501 Chester Road,
Manchester, Lancashire M16 9HH
Neil Mutch

CheethamBellJWT
0161 832 8884
www.jwt.com
Astley House, Quay Street,
Manchester, Lancashire M3 4AS
Dave Barraclough

Citigate Albert Frank
020 7282 8000
www.citigateaf.co.uk
26 Finsbury Square,
London EC2A 1SH
Paul Anderson

Citigate SMARTS
0131 555 0425
www.smarts.co.uk
100 Ocean Drive,
Edinburgh EH6 6JJ
Hilary Joiner / Colin Montgomery

Clark McKay Walpole
020 7487 9750
www.cmw-uk.com
42-46 Weymouth Street,
Marylebone, London W1G 6NR
Steve Walpole via Jula Lewsey

**Clear Marketing
Communications**
0161 448 8008
www.clearmarketing.co.uk
121 Palatine Road, Didsbury,
Manchester M20 3YA
Tony Price / Chris Doyle

Clemmow Hornby Inge
020 7025 8989
www.chiadvertising.com
3rd Floor, Paramount House,
162-170 Wardour Street,
London W1F 8ZX
Brian Turner / Micky Tudor /
Matt Pam

Cogent
0121 627 5040
www.cogent.co.uk
Heath Farm, Hampton Lane,
Meriden, West Midlands CV7 7LL
Ann Smith

Cognition
01926 330800
www.cognitionbnt.com
4 Dormer Place, Leamington Spa,
Warwickshire CV32 5AE
Peter Hughes

Comma
020 7935 4554
www.comma.co.uk
12 Dorset Street,
London W1U 6QS
Jane Marr

**Corporate Marketing and
Advertising Services**
01608 811228
www.cmas.co.uk
The Granary, Southill, Cornbury
Park, Charlbury, Oxford OX7 3EW
Andy Spilsbury

**Crammond Dickens Lerner &
Partners merged with ideas
eurobrand**
020 7240 8100
www.cdl-uk.com
1 Earlham Street,
London WC2H 9LL
Barnaby Dickens / Jeremy
Jackson-Sytner

Cravens Advertising
0191 232 6683
www.cravens.co.uk
42 Leazes Park Road,
Newcastle upon Tyne NE1 4PL
Alan Harvey

Creative Marketing Services
0870 381 6222
www.cmsadvertising.co.uk
CMS House, 4 Spring Bank Place,
Bradford, West Yorkshire BD8 7BX
Chris Hughes

Creative Media Advertising
01260 292600
www.creativenet.co.uk
Overton House, West Road,
Congleton, Cheshire CW12 1JY
Rob Simpson

Cuba Advertising
020 7637 3786
www.cubaadvertising.co.uk
15 Little Portland Street,
London W1W 8BW
Carl Harris

DDB London
020 7258 3979
www.ddblondon.com
12 Bishops Bridge Road,
London W2 6AA
Ruth Harlow

**Delaney Lund Knox Warren &
Partners**
020 7836 3474
www.dlkw.co.uk
25 Wellington Street,
London WC2E 7DA
Debbie Simmonds

Dewynters PLC
020 7321 0488
www.dewynters.com
48 Leicester Square,
London WC2H 7QD
Bob King

**Different Advertising, Design &
Marketing**
0191 261 0111
www.different-uk.com
10 Summerhill Terrace,
Newcastle upon Tyne NE4 6EB
Chris Rickaby / Mark Martin

Doner Cardwell Hawkins
020 7734 0511
www.doner.co.uk
26-34 Emerald Street,
London WC1N 3QA
Paul Cardwell

Dowcarter
020 7689 1200
www.dowcarter.com
48 Rawstorne Street,
London EC1V 7ND
Kelvin Tillinghast

Duckworth Finn Grubb Waters
020 7734 5888
www.dfgw.com
41 Great Pulteney Street,
London W1F 9NZ
Helen Jordan

Edmonds Advertising
0131 467 8333
www.edmonds.co.uk
23 Mitchell Street,
Edinburgh EH6 7BD
David Cowan / Marion Mclaren

EHS Brann
020 7017 1000
www.ehsbrann.com
6 Briset Street, Clerkenwell,
London EC1M 5NR
Zoe Beer

Ellison Communications
020 7510 5900
www.ellisoncommunications.co.uk
The Media Building, 5 Selsdon
Way, London E14 9GL
Glenn Portch

Emberton Dale Advertising
01908 668338
www.emberton-dale.com
224 Upper Fifth Street,
Central Milton Keynes,
Buckinghamshire MK9 2HR
John Emberton /
Richard Hackman

Emery McLaven Orr
01793 767300
www.emo.uk.com
The Old Rectory, Vicarage Lane,
Highworth, Swindon SN6 7AD
PJ Lane

uro RSCG London
020 7467 9200
www.partnersbddh.co.uk
15 Alfred Place, London WC1 7EB
Kirsty Shaw

EURO RSCG Wnek
020 7240 4111
www.eurorscg.co.uk
Gosper, Cuploa House, No.15
Alfred Place, London WC1E 7EB
Nick Casing

Factor 3 Communications
01242 254242
www.factor3.co.uk
Royal House, Parabola Road,
Cheltenham,
Gloucestershire GL50 3AH
Nick Fairburn

Fallon
020 7494 9120
www.fallon.co.uk
67-69 Beak Street,
London W1F 9SW
Mark Elwood

Family Advertising Limited
0131 220 7100
www.familyadvertising.co.uk
CBC, House 24, Canning Street,
Edinburgh EH3 8EG
David Isaac / Kevin Bird

FCB London
020 7947 8000
www.london.fcb.com
55 Newman Street,
London W1T 3EB
Rachael Sanderson

Feel
020 7359 9600
www.feelagency.com
1 Mercer Street, Covent Garden,
London WC2H 9QJ
Chris Arnold

Fire IMC
02890 774388
www.fireimc.com
10 Dargan Crescent,
Belfast BT3 9JP
Adrian Power

The names included are contacts for junior creative positions and work placements

Flint
020 7851 7800
www.flint.uk.com
50 Marshall Street,
London W1F 9BQ
Jane Maskell

Fox Kalomaski
020 7691 8090
www.foxkalomaski.co.uk
48 Fitzroy Street,
London W1T 5BS
Nicola Wright

Fox Murphy
01603 621587
www.foxmurphy.co.uk
17-19 St Georges Street,
Norwich NR3 1AB
Rob Young / Chris Haynes

Frame C
0141 559 5840
www.framecunningham.co.uk
100 Brunswick Street,
Glasgow G1 1TF
Neil Wallace

frank the agency
01625 521444
www.itsfrank.com
Camellia House, 76 Water Lane,
Wilmslow, Cheshire SK9 5BB
Carl Edwards

GCAS Advertising
028 9032 3418
www.gcasgroup.com
Russell Court, 38-52 Lisburn
Road, Belfast, N Ireland BT9 6AA
Peter Ellis

Genesis Advertising
028 9031 3344
www.genesis-advertising.co.uk
7 Crescent Gardens, Belfast,
Northern Ireland BT7 1NS
Nigel Jameson

Gillett & Bevan
0161 228 0023
www.gillett-bevan.com
5 Richmond Street, Manchester,
Lancashire M1 3HF
Nigel Rayner

Gough Allen Stanley
01527 579555
www.gough.co.uk
Kembrey House, 5 Worcester
Road, Bromsgrove,
Worcestershire B61 7DL
Sue Bailey

Grey London
020 7636 3399
www.grey.com
215-227 Great Portland Street,
London W1W 5PN
Polly Varnes

GSB Associates
01323 722933
www.gsba.co.uk
31 St Leonards Road, Eastbourne,
East Sussex BN21 4SE
Ian Golledge

Guy Robertson Partnership
0141 341 2800
www.grpartnership.co.uk
11 Ashley Street, Glasgow G3 6DR
Guy Robertson

Hay Smith Advertising
0131 623 3200
www.haysmith.co.uk
15 Mentone Gardens,
Edinburgh EH9 2DJ
Trevor Hay

HDM Agency
020 7321 2227
www.hdmagency.co.uk
151 Shaftesbury Avenue,
London WC2 8LA
Dave Ditzel

**Healthworld Communications
Group**
020 7262 2141
www.healthworld.co.uk
121-141 Westbourne Terrace,
London W2 6JR
Aimee Watson

HHCL/Red Cell
020 7436 3333
www.ehhcl.net
5th Floor, Kent House, 14-17
Market Place, London W1W 8AJ
Jonathan Burley via Lisa Hall

Hicklin Slade & Partners
0207 664 0404
www.hicklinslade.com
Bewlay House, 2 Swallow Place,
London W1B 2AE
Malcolm Cauldwell /
Adam Hayward

Hird Advertising
0114 266 5289
Omega Court, 376 Cemetery
Road, Sheffield S11 8FT
Jeff Noake

HPS Group
01494 684300
www.hpsgroup.co.uk
Park House, Desborough Park
Road, High Wycombe,
Buckinghamshire HP12 3DJ
Steve Kendall /
Jane Von Klemperer

Huet & Co
0161 835 3100
www.huet.co.uk
1st Floor, 5 Ridgefield,
Manchester M2 6EG
Michel Huet

Image Group Jersey
01534 734444
www.image.gg
1 West Centre, Bath Street,
St Helier, Jersey JE3 4FB
Glen Smith / Andrew Lewis

J. Walter Thompson
020 7656 7000
www.jwt.co.uk
1 Knightsbridge Green,
London SW1X 7NW
Katy Whinder

Karmarama
020 7612 1777
www.karmarama.com
Level 5, 16 Gresse Street,
London W1T 1QL
Naresh Ramchandani /
Dave Buonaguidi

Kinghorn-Davies Advertising
0191 261 8666
www.kinghorn-davies.co.uk
35-39 Blandford Square,
Newcastle upon Tyne,
Tyne And Wear NE1 4HW
Terry Wilson

Langham Works
020 7636 5552
www.langhamworks.co.uk
32 Gosfield Street,
London W1V 6ED
Gareth John

Leagas Delaney
020 7758 1758
www.leagasdelaney.com
1 Alfred Place, London WC1E 7EB
Rob Burleigh

Leith Edinburgh
0131 561 8600
www.leith.co.uk
37 The Shore, Leith,
Edinburgh EH6 6QU
Gerry Farrell

Leith London
020 7758 1400
www.leith.co.uk
1-4 Vigo Street, London W1S 3HT
John Messum / Simon Bere

Leo Burnett
020 7751 1800
www.leoburnett.com
Warwick Building, Avonmore
Road, Kensington Village,
London W14 8HQ
Alex Plumle

Interfocus Advertising
01622 767 700
www.interfocus.uk.com
Media House, 1 James Whatman
Court, Ashford Road, Maidstone,
Kent ME14 5PP
Roberta Light

LMA
023 8077 2888
www.lma.co.uk
LMA House, 3rd Avenue,
Southampton,
Hampshire SO15 0LD
Ed Chesterton / Colin Lewis

Love Creative
0161 907 3150
www.lovecreative.com
72 Tib Street, Manchester M4 1LG
Phil Skegg

Lowe
020 7584 5033
www.loweuk.com
60 Sloane Avenue,
London SW3 3XB
Ed Morris

Lyle Bailie International
028 9033 1044
www.lylebailie.com
31 Bruce St, Great Victoria St,
Belfast BT2 7JD
Julie Anne Bailie

M&C Saatchi
020 7543 4500
www.mcsaatchi.com
36 Golden Square,
London W1F 9EE
Julie Mirfakhraee

Maher Bird Associates
020 7309 7200
www.mba.co.uk
82 Charing Cross Road,
London WC2H 0BA
Lin Bolton / Graham Kerr

Marr Associates
0131 555 4040
www.marr.co.uk
Waterside House, 46 The Shore,
Leith, Edinburgh EH6 6QU
Colin Marr

Marten Gibbon Associates
020 7340 1900
www.mga-advertising.co.uk
11 Little College Street,
London SW1P 3SH
Ed Pollard

Martin Tait Redheads
0191 232 1926
www.mtra.co.uk
Buxton House Buxton Street,
Newcastle upon Tyne NE1 6NJ
Colette Maddison

McCann Erickson
020 7837 3737
www.mccann-erickson.co.uk
7 Herbrand Street,
London WC1N 1EX
Nicky O'Malley

McCann Erickson Birmingham
0121 7133500
www.mccann-erickson.co.uk
McCann House, Highlands Road,
Shirley, Solihull B90 4WE
Alison Richards

McCann Erickson Bristol
0117 921 1764
www.mccann-erickson.co.uk
6 King Street, Bristol BS1 4EQ
John Hayward

McCann Erickson Manchester
01625 822200
www.mccann-erickson.co.uk
Bonis Hall Prestbury,
Macclesfield, Cheshire SK10 4EF
Tracey Harman

Mearns & Gill
01224 646311
www.mearns-gill.freeserve.co.uk
7 Carden Place,
Aberdeen AB10 1PP
Alan Mearns

Miles Calcraft Briginshaw Duffy
020 7073 6900
www.mcbd.co.uk
15 Rathbone Street,
London W1T 1NB
Zorrica Blackley

Mortimer Whittaker O'Sullivan
020 7379 8844
www.mwo.co.uk
The Carriage Hall, 29 Floral
Street, London WC2E 9TD
Shauna O'Donnell

Mother
020 7012 1999
www.motherlondon.com
Biscuit Building, 10 Redchurch
Street, London E2 7DD
Teddy George

Mustoes
020 7379 9999
www.mustoes.co.uk
2-4 Bucknall Street,
London WC2H 8LA
Mick Mahoney

Navigator Blue
028 9024 6722
www.navigatorblue.com
The Baths, 18 Ormeau Avenue,
Belfast, Northern Ireland BT2 8HS
Terry Corr / Connor Kelly

Nexus/H UK
01892 517777
www.nexus-h.co.uk
Multimedia House, Hill Street,
Tunbridge Wells, Kent TN1 2BY
Rita Kopiel

NMI Group
020 7436 5000
www.nmigroup.com
Middlesex House,
34-42 Cleveland Street,
London W1T 4JE

Ogilvy & Mather
020 7345 3000
www.ogilvy.com
10 Cabot Square, Canary Wharf,
London E14 4QB
Annie Scott / Gemma Wise /
Sinead Ryan / Sadie Joy /
Melissa Wilmot

Ogilvy Primary Contact
020 7468 6900
www.primary.co.uk
5 Theobald's Road,
London WC1X 8SH
Roger Gallucci

OgilvyOne Worldwide
020 7566 7000
www.ogilvy.com
10 Cabot Square, Canary Wharf,
London E14 4QB
Annie Scott / Gemma Wise /
Sinead Ryan / Sadie Joy /
Melissa Wilmot

Omobono
01223 307 000
www.omobono.co.uk
Old Farm Business Centre, Church
Road, Toft, Cambridge CB3 7RF
Chris Butterworth

Poulter Partners
0113 285 6500
www.poultergroup.com
Rose Wharf, East Street, Leeds,
West Yorkshire LS9 8EE
Corrine Pujara

Profero
020 7387 2000
www.profero.com
Centro 3, Mandela St,
London N1 0DU
Tina Brazil

Proximity London
020 7479 8000
www.proximitylondon.com
191 Old Marylebone Road,
London NW1 5DW
Diane Smart

Publicis
020 7935 4426
www.publicis.co.uk
82 Baker Street,
London W1U 6AE
Ingrid Osborne-Holst

PWLC
0113 398 0120
www.pwlc.uk.com
46 The Calls, Leeds, West
Yorkshire LS2 7EY
Pete Camponi / Rick Ward

Quiet Storm
020 7907 1140
www.quietstorm.co.uk
15-16 Margaret Street,
London W1W 8RW
Becky Clarke / Rashel Taschian

Radford Creative Communications
0161 832 8807
www.radfordnet.com
Blackfriars House, Parsonage,
Manchester M3 2JA
Phil Atkinson

Radioville
020 7534 5959
www.radioville.co.uk
143 Wardour Street,
London W1F 8WA
Tim Craig

Rainey Kelly Campbell Roalfe/Y&R
020 7404 2700
www.uk.yr.com
Greater London House,
Hampstead Road,
London NW1 7QP
Kate Pozzi

Rhythmm
0117 942 9786
www.rhythmm.co.uk
Trelawny House, Surrey Street,
Bristol, Avon BS2 8PS
Kevin Young

RLA Southern
01202 297755
www.rla.co.uk
Burlington House,
Old Christchurch Road,
Bournemouth, Dorset BH1 2HZ
Sean Millard

Robson Brown
0191 232 2443
www.robson-brown.co.uk
Clavering House, Clavering Place,
Newcastle upon Tyne NE1 3NG
Angela Foley

Rock Kitchen Harris
0116 233 7500
www.rkh.co.uk
The Creative Mill, 31 Lower Brown
Street, Leicester,
Leicestershire LE1 5TH
Paul Petherick / Tracy Scott

Heresy Group
020 7349 6800
www.roose.co.uk
102 Sydney Street,
London SW3 6NJ
Mandy Enright

Ross Levenson Harris
020 8390 4611
www.rlh.co.uk
60-63 Victoria Road, Surbiton,
Surrey KT6 4NQ
Christine Jones

RPM3
020 7434 4343
www.rpm3.co.uk
William Blake House, 8 Marshall
Street, London W1V 2AJ
Russell Wales

Saatchi & Saatchi
020 7636 5060
www.saatchi.com
80 Charlotte Street,
London W1T 4QP
Tracy Flaherty

The names included are contacts for junior creative positions and work placements

Sans Frontiere Marketing
01273 487800
www.sansfrontiere.co.uk
73 High Street, Lewes,
East Sussex BN4 1XG
Audrey Evans

Sass
01565 832 832
www.puresass.com
The Haybarn, Mere Hall Park,
Warrington Road, Mere,
Cheshire WA16 0PY
Graham Sass

Scholz & Friends London
020 7961 4090
www.scholzandfriends.co.uk
80 Clerkenwell Road,
London EC1M 5RJ
Steve Spence / Trevor Kennedy

Sellers & Rogers
0115 955 1159
www.sel-rog.co.uk
Price House, 37 Stoney Street,
The Lace Market,
Nottingham NG1 1LS
David Spence

Seriously Bright
020 7494 2677
www.seriouslybright.com
William Blake House,
8 Marshall Street,
London W1F 7EJ
David Delmonte

Severn Advertising
01905 795999
www.severnad.co.uk
Severn House, 30 Ombersley
Street, West Droitwich Spa,
Worcestershire WR9 8QX
Kieran Fitzpatrick

Smee's Advertising
020 7486 6644
www.smees.co.uk
3-5 Duke Street, London W1M 6BA
Anthony Smee

Solus Strategic
01624 666 000
www.solus-strategic.com
28 Victoria Street, Douglas,
Isle of Man IM1 2LE

Soul
020 7292 5999
www.souladvertising.com
4 New Burlington Street,
Mayfair, London W1F 2JD
Ruth Croutch

St Lukes
020 7380 8888
www.stlukes.co.uk
22 Dukes Road,
London WC1H 9PN
Zoe Roberts

Stuart Hirst
0113 243 4646
www.stuarthirst.demon.co.uk
Chelwood House, 35 Chelwood
Drive, Leeds, LS8 2AT
Mike Wappett

**Target Marketing
Communications**
01242 633100
www.targetgroup.co.uk
Brand House, 62 Painswick Rd,
Cheltenham,
Gloucestershire GL50 2EU
Sharron Rudge / Joey Doran

TBWA\London
020 7573 6666
www.tbwa-london.com
76-80 Whitfield Street,
London W1T 4EZ

Team Saatchi
020 7436 6636
www.teamsaatchi.co.uk
23 Howland Street,
London W1T 4AY
Mike Middleton

Ten Alps MTD
0131 553 9200
www.tenalpsmtd.com
Great Michael House, 14 Links
Place, Edinburgh EH6 7EZ
Euan Carmichael

The Brahm Agency
0113 230 4000
www.brahm.com
The Brahm Building, Alma Road,
Headingley, Leeds LS6 2AH
Maria Lambert

The Bridge
0141 552 8384
www.thebridgeuk.com
The Jacobean Building , 49/53
Virginia Street, Glasgow G1 1TS
Jonathan D'Aguilar

The JJ Group
01865 343100
www.thejjgroup.com
Little Baldon House, Little Baldon,
Oxford, Oxfordshire OX44 9PU
Sue Ingledew

**The Levy McCallum Advertising
Agency**
0141 248 7977
www.levymccallum.co.uk
203 Saint Vincent Street,
Glasgow G2 5NH
Roy L. McCallum

Freshwater
029 20 729400
Freshwater House, Cardiff Gate
Businees Park, Cardiff, CF23 8RS
Johnny Chau

The Thinking Agency
0113 289 0000
www.clarendon-am.co.uk
Carlton House, Pickering
Street, Leeds LS12 2QG
James Eate

The Union Advertising Agency
0131 625 6000
www.union.co.uk
Union House, 18 Inverleith
Terrace, Edinburgh EH3 5NS
Don Smith

The Works London
020 8233 1600
www.theworkslondon.com
2-3 Melbray Mews, 158
Hurlingham Road,
London SW6 3NS
Josh Robinson / Debra Ogilvie

Times Right Marketing
01293 772111
www.trm.co.uk
Suite 6F, Gatwick House,
Peeks Brook Lane,
Horley, Surrey RH6 9ST
John Gallie

**Vallance Carruthers Coleman
Priest**
020 7255 0200
www.vccp.com
Greencoat House,
15 Francis Street, Victoria,
London SW1P 1DH
Caroline Palmer

Wallis Tomlinson
0121 233 9494
www.waltom.co.uk
36-37 Cox Street,
St Paul's Square, Birmingham,
West Midlands B3 1RD
Geoff Tomlinson

Walsh Trott Chick Smith
020 7907 1200
www.wtcs.co.uk
Holden House, 57 Rathbone
Place, London W1T 1JU
Dave Trott / Gordon Smith

Ware Anthony Rust
01223 566212
www.war.uk.com
Newnham Mill, Newnham Road,
Cambridge CB3 9EY
Dale Haste / Richard Bland

WCRS
020 7806 5000
www.wcrs.co.uk
5 Golden Square,
London W1F 9BS
Sophia Cliffe

Wieden & Kennedy
020 7299 7523
www.wk.com
16 Hanbury Street,
London E1 6QR
Matt Gooden / Ben Walker

Willox Ambler Rodford Law
020 7400 0900
www.warl.co.uk
30-32 Gray's Inn Road,
London WC1X 8HR
Tommy Adkins

**Woodreed Creative
Consultancy**
01892 515025
www.woodreed.com
49 The Pantiles,
Tunbridge Wells, Kent TN2 5TE
George Campbell

Woolley Pau
020 7836 6060
www.letsgotowork.com
36-37 Maiden Lane,
London WC2E 7LJ
Dean Woolley

WWAV Rapp Collins
020 8735 8000
www.wwavrc.co.uk
1 Riverside, Manbre Road,
London W6 9WA
Andy Wilson / Ian Hayworth

Agency Republic
020 7942 0000
www.agencyrepublic.com
1 Battersea Bridge Rd,
London SW11 3BZ
Darren Andrew

Agency.com
020 7964 8200
www.agency.com
85 Strand, London WC2R 0DW
Gemma Ellis

AKQA
020 7494 9200
www.akqa.com
Prince's House, 38 Jermyn Street,
London SW1Y 6DN
Daniel Bonner

Amaze
0870 240 1700
www.amaze.com
Kings Court, Manor Farm Road,
Runcorn, Cheshire, WA7 1HR
Helen Watson / Joanne Kirshaw

Arc Interactive
020 7071 2692
www.arcinteractive.co.uk
Warwick Building, Kensington
Village, Avonmore Rd,
London W14 8HQ
Natt Watt

Arnold Interactive
020 7908 2700
www.arnoldinteractive.com
14 Welbeck Street,
London W1G 9XU
Maxine Gregson

Aspect Group
020 7504 6900
www.aspectgroup.co.uk
Clerkenwell House, 67
Clerkenwell Road,
London EC1R 5BL
Hilary Wilkie

Atticmedia
020 7490 8789
www.atticmedia.com
34 Waterside, 44-48 Wharf Road,
Islington, London N1 7UX
Ross Baird

Beech2
020 7297 9497
www.beech2.com
Medius House, 2 Sheraton Street,
London W1F 8BH
Derek Hayes

Big Picture Interactive
01926 422002
www.bigpictureinteractive.co.uk
9 Parade, Leamington Spa,
Warwickshire, CV32 4DG
Becky Dempsey

Brave Marketing
020 7471 1984
www.brave.co.uk
The Blue Building, Fulham Island,
40 Vanston Place,
London SW6 1AX
Beri Cheatham

Carlson Digital
020 8875 0875
www.carlson-europe.com
Carlson Court, 116 Putney Bridge
Road, London SW15 2NQ
Matt Hall

Chemistry Communications
020 7736 5355
www.chemistrygroup.co.uk
158 Hurlingham Road, Melbray
Mews, Fulham, London SW6 3NG
Denise Myers

Cimex Inc
020 7359 4664
www.cimex.com
53-55 Scrutton Street,
London EC2A 4XL
Az Mohammed

CMW Interactive
020 7224 4050
www.cmwinteractive.com
42-46 Weymouth Street,
Marylebone, London W1G 6NR
Julia Lewsey

Conchango
01784 222222
www.conchango.com
Heritage House, Church Road,
Egham, Surrey TW20 9QD
Charlotte Cook

Craik Jones Digital
020 7734 1650
www.digital.craikjones.co.uk
120 Regent Street,
London W1B 5RY
Mark Buckingham / Lee Roberts /
David Brown / Rebecca Rae

Cramm Francis Woolf
020 7539 7780
www.cfw.co.uk
12 Burleigh Street,
London WC2E 7PX
Lindsay Watson

cScape
020 7689 8800
www.cscape.com
4 Pear Tree Court, Clerkenwell,
London EC1R 0DS
Para Mullan

Dare Digital
020 7612 3600
www.daredigital.com
8-10 Great Titchfield Street,
London W1W 8BB
Flo Heiss

Digit
020 7684 6769
www.digitlondon.com
6 Corbet Place, Spitalfields,
London E1 6NH
Daljit Singh

Digitas Europe
020 7494 6700
www.digitas.com
183 Eversholt Street,
London NW1 1BU
Louisa Norrie / Lifette Brown

Digiterre
020 7381 7910
www.digiterre.com
The Quadrangle, 49 Atalanta
Street, London SW6 6TU
Ian Murran

DLKW Dialogue
020 7836 3474
www.dlkwdialogue.com
25 Wellington Street,
London WC2E 7DA
Debbie Simmonds

DNA
020 7357 0573
www.dna.co.uk
2&7 Brewary Square, Butlers
Wharf, London SE1 2LF
Joe Marvell

Domino Systems
01865 821821
www.domino.com
The Innovation Centre, Kingston
Bagpuize, Oxfordshire OX13 5AP
Hannah Woodley

Dowcarter
020 7689 1200
www.dowcarter.com
48 Rawstorne Street,
London EC1V 7ND
Kelvin Tillinghast

DVA
01256 882032
www.dva.co.uk
7/8 Campbell Court, Bramley,
Tadley, Hampshire RG26 5EG
Barry Gibson

E3 Media
01179 021333
www.e3media.co.uk
2nd Floor, The Tobacco Factory,
Raleigh Rd, Southville,
Bristol BS3 1TF
Wesley Hogg

EHS Brann
020 7017 1000
www.ehsbrann.com
6 Briset Street, London EC1M 5NR
Lu Dixon / Trevor Chambers

Equator
0141 229 1800
www.eqtr.com
Sovereign House, 58 Elliot
Street, Glasgow G3 8DZ
James Jefferson

The names included are contacts for junior creative positions and work placements

Exponetic
020 7613 1053
www.exponetic.com
5/51 Derbyshire Street, Bethnal
Green, London E2 6JQ
James Bebbington

Fernhart New Media
020 8253 0210
www.fernhart.com
77 Park Lane, Croydon CR0 1JG
Bryan Mann

Freestyle New Media Group
01926 652832
www.fsnm.co.uk
The American Barns, Banbury Rd,
Lighthorne,
Warwickshire CV35 0AE
Tracy Prince

Global Beach
020 7384 1188
www.globalbeach.com
522 Fulham Road,
London SW6 5NR

Glue London
020 7739 2345
www.gluelondon.com
31 Old Nichol Street,
London E2 7HR
Sebastian Royce

Good Technology
020 7565 0022
www.goodtechnology.com
332b Ladbroke Grove,
London W10 5AH
Sezannah Saffet

Graphico New Media
01635 522810
www.graphico.co.uk
Goldwell House, Old Bath Road,
Newbury, Berkshire RG14 1JH
Andrew Holden

Greenroom Digital
020 7426 5147
www.greenroom-digital.com
120-124 Curtain Road,
London EC2A 3SQ
Jon Hamm

Groovy Train
020 7748 6634
www.groovytrain.com
Business Design Centre,
52 Upper Street, London N1 0QH
Paul Grier

Gurus
020 8838 3007
www.gurus.co.uk
4 Park Royal Metro Centre,
Britannia Way, London NW10 7PA
Nasir Ahmed

Head to Head Web
020 8392 2022
www.headtohead.net
107 Mortlake High Street,
London SW14 8HQ
Francois Reynier

Hi-Res
020 7729 3090
www.hi-res.net
8-9 Rivington Place,
London EC2A 3BA
Amy Harrison

IDNet
01462 476555
www.idnet.net
The Spirella Building,
Letchworth, Herts SG6 4ET.
Andy Field

Inbox Media
01793 348880
www.inbox.co.uk
Contact House, High Street,
Wanborough, Swindon SN4 0AE
Gary Stevens

Incepta Online
020 7282 2800
www.inceptaonline.com
3 London Wall Buildings, London
Wall, London EC2M 5SY
Isobel Palmer

Intercea
01189 169900
www.intercea.co.uk
1 Transcentral, Bennet Road,
Reading, Berkshire RG2 0QX
Jan Watson

Interesource
020 7613 8200
www.interesource.co.uk
50-52 Paul Street,
London EC2A 4LB
Ian Howlett / Tim Malbon

IR Group
020 7436 3140
www.ir-group.com
PO Box 4387, 6-10 Great Portland
Street, London W1A 7SP
Hilla Neske

IS Solutions
01932 893333
www.issolutions.co.uk
Windmill House, 91-93 Windmill
Road, Sunbury-on-Thames,
Middlesex TW16 7EF
Jean Bushell

Javelin Group
020 7961 3200
www.javelingroup.com
165 Fleet Street,
London EC4A 2DY
Terry Jones

Joshua Interactive
020 7453 7900
www.joshua-agency.co.uk
Wells Point, 79 Wells Street,
London W1T 3QN
Mitch Levy / Jo Eggleston

Kleber Design
020 7729 2819
www.kleber.net
3rd Floor, 95A Rivington Street,
London EC2A 3AY

KMP Associates
08708 688900
www.kmpassociates.com
Kingfisher Court, Yew Street,
Stockport, Cheshire SK4 2HG
Bill Daring / John Keefe

Lateral
020 7613 4449
www.lateral.net
Charlotte House, 47-49 Charlotte
Road, London EC2A 3QT
Su Sareen / Colin Douglas

Lawton eMarketing
023 8082 8500
www.lawtonemarketing.com
4 Grosvenor Square,
Southampton SO15 2BE
Sarah Hornby

Lean Mean Fighting Machine
020 7722 4988
www.lmfm.co.uk
Primrose Hill Business Centre,
110 Gloucester Avenue,
London NW1 8JA
Dave Bedwood

Lightmaker
01892 615015
www.lightmaker.com
Century Place, Buildings 3 & 4,
Lamberts Road,
Tunbridge Wells, Kent TN2 3EH
Sophie Campbell

Linney Design
01623 450460
www.linneydesign.com
Adamsway, Mansfield,
Nottinghamshire NG18 4FL
John Kay

McCann-I
01625 822200
www.mccann-i.com
Bonis Hall, Bonis Hall Lane,
Prestbury, Cheshire SK10 4EF
Tracy Harman

M-Corp
01425 477766
www.m-corp.com
Somerley, Ringwood,
Hampshire BH24 3PL
Chris Murdoch

Mitchell Conner Searson
020 7420 7991 / 0115 9596 455
www.broadband.co.uk
151 Shaftesbury Avenue,
London WC2H 8AL
Ian Malone

Modem Media UK
020 7874 9400
www.modemmedia.com
183 Eversholt Street,
London NW1 1BU
Louisa Norrie / Lifette Brown

Moonfish
08700 70 4321
www.moonfish.com
2 Sheraton Street,
London W1F 8BH
Robert Pinfold

NetInfo
01628 687800
www.netinfo.com
Berkshire House, Queen Street,
Maidenhead, Berkshire SL6 1NF
Carl Groth

Nucleus
020 8398 9133
www.nucleus.co.uk
John Loftus House,
Summer Road, Thames Ditton,
Surrey KT7 0RD
Suzanne Lykiard

Object1 / LB Icon
020 7684 1800
www.object1.com
6-8 Standard Place, Rivington
Street, London EC2A 3BE
Brett Bircham

Ogilvy Interactive
020 7345 3000
www.ogilvy.com
10 Cabot Square, Canary Wharf,
London E14 4GB
Siobhann Carolan

Oyster Partners
020 7446 7500
www.oyster.com
1 Naorojl Street,
London WC1X 0JD
Claire Myerson

Pilot Interactive
0113 228 2359
www.pilotinteractive.co.uk
Devonshire Hall, Devonshire
Avenue, Street Lane,
Leeds LS8 1AW
Chris Hemingway

Poke
020 7749 5353
www.pokelondon.com
Biscuit Building, 10 Redchurch
Street, London E2 7DD
Lizzie Underwood

Poulter Partners
0113 285 6500
www.poultergroup.com
Rose Wharf, East Street,
Leeds LS9 8EE
Sally Gaunt / Corinne Pujara

Precedent Communications
020 7216 1300
www.precedent.co.uk
109-123 Clifton Street,
London EC2A 4LD

Preloaded
020 7684 3505
www.preloaded.com
16-24 Underwood Street,
London N1 7JQ
Paul Canty

Profero
020 7387 2000
www.profero.com
Centro & Mandela Street,
London NW1 0DU
Tina Brazil

Proximity London
020 7298 1000
www.proximitylondon.com
191 Old Marylebone Road,
London NW1 5DW
Hazel Malone

Publicis Dialog
020 7935 4426
www.publicis-dialog.co.uk
82 Baker Street, London W1U 6AE
Nick Spudzinski

Reading Room
020 7025 1800
www.readingroom.com
53 Frith St, Soho,
London W1D 4SN
Margaret Manning / Simon Usher

Realise
0131 476 6000
www.realise.com
142 Commercial Street,
Edinburgh EH6 6LB
Andrew Craig

Recollective
020 7064 4196
www.recollective.co.uk
Recollective Limited, Studio 2,
Alaska Building 600, 61 Grange
Road, London SE1 3BB
Frances O'Reilly

Recreate Solutions
020 8233 2916
www.recreatesolutions.com
London House,
271-273 King Street,
Hammersmith, London W6 9LZ
Gigi Bettencourt-Gomes

Redhouse Lane
020 7462 2600
www.redhouselane.co.uk
14-15 Bedford Square,
London WC1B 3JA

Redweb
08451 303010
www.redweb.co.uk
Quay House, The Quay,
Poole, Dorset BH15 1HA
Andrew Henning

Redwood New Media
020 7747 7226
www.redwood-newmedia.com
7 Saint Martin's Place,
London WC2N 4HA

Rufus Leonard
020 7404 4490
www.rufusleonard.com
The Drill Hall, 57A Farringdon
Road, London EC1M 3JB
Steve Howell

Sapient
020 7786 4500
www.sapient.co.uk
1 Bartholomew Lane,
London EC2N 2AX

Framfab
020 7071 6300
www.framfab.com
Elizabeth House, 5th Floor,
39 York Rd, London SE1 7NQ
Lucy Cavallo

Screen Pages
01932 359160
www.screenpages.com
4 The Courtyard, Wisley,
Surrey GU23 6QL
Mark Spires

Sequence
0845 1000 400
www.sequence.co.uk
Sequence, Media Centre, Bridge
Street, Cardiff CF10 2EE
Mark Johnson

Splendid
020 7287 4442
www.howsplendid.com
54-62 Regent Street,
London W1B 9HA
Dan Morris

Swamp
08451 202405
www.swampme.com
103 Clarendon Road,
Leeds, LS2 9DF
Andrew Brown

Syzygy
020 7460 4080
www.syzygy.net
4th Floor, Elsley House, 24-30
Great Titchfield Street,
London W1W 8BF
Rachel Stretch / Kate Riley

TBG
020 7428 6650
www.tbgltd.com
100 Highgate Studios, 53-79
Highgate Road, London NW5 1TL
Kenneth Lillie

TechnoPhobia
0114 221 2123
www.technophobia.co.uk
The Workstation, 15 Paternoster
Row, Sheffield S1 2BX
Andrew Pendrick

Tequila London
020 7440 1100
www.tequila-uk.com
82 Dean Street, London W1D 3HA
Vanessa Kelly

The Big Group
020 7229 8827
www.biginteractive.co.uk
91 Princedale Road, Holland Park,
London W11 4NS

The Hub
020 8560 9222
www.thehub.co.uk
The Power House, 1 Linkfield
Road, Isleworth,
Middlesex TW7 6QG

Thoughtbubble
020 7387 8890
www.thoughtbubble.com
58/60 Fitzroy Street,
London W1T 5BU
Terrance Krjezl

TMG
020 7261 1777
www.tmg.co.uk
36 Southwark Bridge Road,
London SE1 9EU
Simon Gill

Tribal DDB
020 7258 4500
www.tribalddb.co.uk
12 Bishops Bridge Road,
London W2 6AA
Ben Clapp

Unit9
020 7613 3330
www.unit9.com
43-44 Hoxton Square,
London N1 6PB
Piero Frescabaldi

Victoria Real
020 8222 4050
www.victoriareal.com
Shepherds Bush Central,
Charecroft Way, London W14 0EE
Sarah Hindmarsh

WDPA Communications
020 7323 2480
www.wdpa.co.uk
142 New Cavendish Street,
London W1W 6YF

Wheel Group
020 7348 1000
www.wheel.co.uk
Beaumont House, Kensington
Village, Avonmore Road,
London W14 8TS
Dasa Malikova

Wireless Information Network
01494 750500
www.winplc.com
1 Cliveden Office Village,
High Wycombe, Bucks HP12 3YZ
Barbara Green

Write Image
020 7959 5400
www.write-image.com
271 Regent Street,
London W1B 2BP
Marie Ellen Broek

XM London
020 7724 7228
www.xmlondon.com
121-141 Westbourne Terrace,
London W2 6JR
Amy Watson

The names included are contacts for junior creative positions and work placements

this year's briefs

This year's briefs

Introduction

The annual ycn design & communication awards exist to inspire, support and showcase emerging design and communication creatives, and to connect them with the creative industries.

The awards centre around a collection of live briefs, written each year by partnering organisations, and spanning broad creative disciplines. Each brief runs alongside a financial award pool of £2000 and creative placements either at the organisation that wrote it or a leading creative agency.

Work submitted in response to each brief is closely examined by these organisations and agencies before a number of commendations are awarded to the most outstanding submissions. Financial awards and creative placements are allocated among the originators of this commended work. Commended submissions then go forward to a second round of judging, hosted by London College of Fashion to determine which will receive our physical award for creative excellence, designed last year by Nick Crosbie at Inflate, and named a Rocket.

Outstanding work is showcased here in *book*, our annual publication produced in collaboration with John Brown Citrus Publishing, and distributed across education and the creative industries. Work is also showcased online at www.ycnonline.com

How work is assessed and how placements and financial awards are allocated

Work is initially assessed by the organisations that have written the briefs, typically alongside members of the creative agencies that they work with. They closely examine all submissions before shortlisting a number of pieces of work to be formally commended. Award pools and agency placements are then allocated among the originators of the commended submissions, at the discretion of the organisations that wrote the briefs.

This stage will take place over April and May, with commendations being published at www.ycnonline.com, sent to course tutors and sent in writing (with certificates of commendation) to entrants at the end of May 2006.

Second round of judging, London College of Fashion

In July 2006, an exhibition of commended work will be hosted by London College of Fashion. Over a two-week period, figures from across the creative industries will visit the exhibition and select the pieces of the work that they feel to be the best of the year.

At the end of the exhibition, the work that has proven to be the most highly regarded across the board will be awarded with a Rocket, the physical award for emerging creative excellence. Originators of commended work will be invited to visit and take part in stages of the event, further details of which can be found at www.ycnonline.com Also online are full details of all those from the industry who will be involved.

A physical award

Different designers and studios are commissioned to design our physical award, which is bestowed upon the originators of the work deemed to be the best of the year after the second round of judging is complete. The design to have been used for the last two years was by Nick Crosbie at Inflate.

At the time of publication, ycn have invited a number of designers and studios to submit prospective designs for this year's award and this process can be charted at the ycn website.

Eligibility
Submissions are invited from anyone aged 30 years or under at the time of their submission, and not being paid to work in a creative department at the time of their entry. If you are in full-time education, there are no age restrictions.

Entry details
The deadline for submitting work is 6pm on the 24th March 2006.

There is no entry fee to submit work.

All submissions must be sent to: ycn, 1st Floor, 181 Cannon Street Road, London E1 2LX, United Kingdom.

• You may respond to as many of the briefs as you wish.
• All submissions must be in the English language.
• You may submit work as an individual or as a team. Teams can consist of as many people as you wish, but please bear in mind that the creative placements pertinent to each brief will typically be for up to two people.
• Submissions are welcomed from overseas.
• Logos, and other information listed in individual briefs, can be found at www.ycnonline.com

Conditions of submission, entry forms and item labels
Submission forms and labels to affix to your submissions can be found at www.ycnonline.com They must be fully completed. Each item that you submit must be listed upon your submission form.

A label must be attached to each item, and numbered clearly if it forms part of a series.

You must read and agree to the conditions of submission available at www.ycnonline.com before submitting any work.

Use of images under copyright
It is crucial that, if you use images from image banks or other sources where they may be under copyright, you make clear in the space provided on the entry form where you have acquired them. Please be detailed in letting us know exactly where work is from – do not, for example, put 'Google Images'.

Deliverables
Please adhere to the following guidelines governing the submission of work:

• Artwork should be mounted on boards.
• Films, animation and other moving-image work should be in a Mac-readable format on a CD, DVD or zip disk.
• Interactive work should be in a Mac-readable format on a CD, DVD or zip disk.
• If you upload any interactive work, you should supply a full URL and details of any plug-ins needed to view the work.
• Radio scripts should be typed, and any recordings should be submitted on tape, minidisk or as a Mac-readable audio format on a CD or zip disk.
• Any additional support

materials, written or otherwise, should all also be clearly labelled.
• Any models or other potentially fragile submissions should be carefully packaged to avoid damage.
• You may submit as many items as you wish.

Key dates
• Submission deadline: 6pm, 24th March 2006.
• Initial round of examination and assessment: April and May 2006.
• Commendations published at the end of May 2006.
• Second round of judging hosted over 2 weeks by London College of Fashion in June/July 2006.
• Rocket awards announced in July 2006.

Return of work
Work will be available for collection from June 2006. Dates and arrangements for collection will be available at www.ycnonline.com nearer the time.

We appreciate that some will be unable to collect work in person, and may need creative for degree shows. Individual arrangements can be discussed by calling 020 7702 0700 or by emailing workreturns@ycnonline.com

Work that has not been arranged to be collected by the end of September 2006 will be recycled. While absolutely every effort is made to ensure the safety of work, ycn cannot accept responsibility for loss of or damage to work submitted.

The Thinkbox Award for outstanding creativity in television
Full details of the new Thinkbox Award, launching as part of the programme this year, can be found at the end of this section on page 190. Extensive details on how Thinkbox are partnering with ycn to recognise and reward the most innovative creative use of TV can also be found at the ycn website.

Educate previous, existing and non-Ted customers as to why Ted Baker is 'No Ordinary Designer Label'

Background

Ted Baker began as a male shirt brand in 1988 and since then the company has grown steadily, expanded its collections and now sells menswear, womenswear, childrenswear, accessories, footwear, eyewear, fragrances, watches, lingerie and home products.

Ted Baker is obsessed with the details, from the bespoke store fits, to the rather witty messages you may find inside a product. It's these type of details that provide the unique selling proposition for the brand coupled with the eccentric brand personality based around Ted's own.

As Ted has chosen not to use advertising in a traditional sense, the brand has to think creatively about how it communicates. More often than not, all the activity is centred around the retail stores, their window displays and themed promotions. However, Ted is extremely keen to look at other innovative ways of reaching old and new consumers beyond the stores, and so is open to other ideas.

Objective

To create a campaign for Ted Baker that will intrigue those customers indicated above to come in-store. The campaign needs to communicate the stylish and aspirational side of the brand while maintaining the original brand personality. It needs to arouse enough curiosity to make people evaluate and re-evaluate the brand.

Creative requirements

To come up with a creative solution that illustrates how different the brand is now from its early days, and will arouse curiosity in those that are not currently buying Ted Baker. You should demonstrate how your creative concept would be applied to at least three different types of media – one of which must be our in-store window display.

Think 'advertising without advertising'.

As well as your in-store window display, you might like to consider demonstrating your concept using online marketing, promotional giveaways, outdoor guerrilla marketing, ideas for events, or any other medium other than conventional channels such as press, tv, radio and billboards.

Target audience

We want to target 20-35 year olds of both sexes who do not currently shop at Ted Baker. The reasons for this may be that they have not revisited the brand since it's male-orientated beginnings, and they are ignorant about the new product offerings and how much the brand has grown up. These customers are usually working, professionals with a decent disposable income. They are aware of trends, go out to pubs, clubs, bars, festivals, read stylish magazines and want to look cool.

However, they do not want to look too edgy. Ted customers like to look a little bit different, but not too much so they feel on top. They like to wear the clothes and not the other way round. They also like quality and are prepared to pay for it.

Considerations

Consumers are so bored of normal advertising and fashion brands trying to be the next new thing. How can you cut through all of the information and get someone's attention?

Ted's tactics have been to entertain and make customers laugh and we want to continue to do this, but in new and innovative ways.

You should think about how you can entertain the viewer but yet also inform and interest them too. Where would you choose to talk to them? Are there places that aren't already saturated with other brand messages? If you use a medium that is already out there, how can you do it differently from anyone else?

Things to remember

It's not simply about using models and collections, think about the brand essence and try to communicate that more effectively.

Remember the acid test: if you remove the logo from the visual, can you still tell what company is behind it?

Always think about PR, would your idea generate media interest which may in turn lead to editorial?

Tone of voice / Brand personality

Quirky
'Out of the ordinary'
Quintessentially British
Witty
Visual humour

Mandatories

The Ted Baker logo should appear on the creative work somewhere. This logo is available in the Ted Baker project pack at www.ycnonline.com

Additional information

www.tedbaker.co.uk

Deliverables

You should adhere to the main deliverables guidelines at the start of this section. These guidelines can also be found at www.ycnonline.com

Judging of work and award information

Work will initially be examined by a team consisting of the closest man to Ted, Ray Kelvin, Ted's Brand Communication Director, Craig Smith and Ted's Marketing Manager, Sushma Sagar. They will prepare a shortlist of work for commendation and allocate their award pool and agency placements accordingly and at their discretion.

Commended submissions will go forward to the second round of judging to be hosted by London College of Fashion in July 2006. Further information on judging can be found at the start of this section and at www.ycnonline.com

TED BAKER
LONDON

Conceive an identity for a new TV channel produced entirely by its viewers, and bring the identity to life by showing it in context

Background

Zip Television is launching a brand-new TV channel, which will push the boundaries of television, providing a new experience for viewers and advertisers. The channel's contents, from idents to programming, will be provided entirely by the viewer. With access to recording devices, from cameras on mobile phones to full edit suites on home computers, viewers will be able to create their own content and tell their own stories.

This community channel will have a schedule packed with programmes about travel, fashion, gigs, alternative lifestyles, careers, health, gardening, exams, local issues and politics; in fact anything that people are passionate about! The content can be contributed as footage, stills, even mobile phone clips.

Within the channel's schedule there will be no traditional TV advertising. The channel will, however, be fully interactive, allowing viewers who press the red button to watch a number of adverts related to the channel's content or advertiser-sponsored channels. The depth of content behind the red button will be significant. Although primarily a TV channel, viewers will be encouraged to use other touchpoints including the web and mobile to engage, connect and communicate with the brand.

Creative Objective

a) To conceive and design a brand identity for this channel, which is simple yet expressive; distinctive yet flexible. The channel should have a name and a logo, something that can be reworked in multiple ways, such as BBC 2's '2' and BBC 3's slugs. The brand identity should be strong enough to work across other media.

b) To design supporting materials that bring your identity to life. You might want to consider how your brand identity would be applied to the 'on channel' interface, and how such an interface and its navigation would best work so that viewers have easy access to all the content on offer. In addition to this, or alternatively, you could create promotional materials that would compel people both to watch the channel and to contribute to the channel's community. How you go about demonstrating how your identity would work is being kept deliberately broad, so you should feel free to use any medium or combination of media you choose.

Target audience

The Channel should have most appeal to viewers aged 16-30, although this is not exclusive. We want viewers who are willing and able to contribute to the channel, sharing their everyday stories and ideas.

What is the essence of the Brand?

The channel is about inclusivity, sharing and the moment. It's about now, right now. It's about taking a photo, texting it and seeing in on screen instantly.

Considerations

When considering the brief, you should consider and research what makes people contribute to message boards and text responses to TV shows. It's not just about how they can interact; it's about WHY they interact. The commercial side of the channel is based on advertiser participation behind the red button. Any interface design must actively encourage viewers to press red.

Media

All TV designs should be presented as though being broadcast on the live channel. The media you use for materials to promote the channel is entirely up to you, although you should keep in mind that the most important word in this brief is "interact".

Additional information

The Zip TV project pack at www.ycnonline.com

Deliverables

You should adhere to the main deliverables guidelines at the start of this section. These guidelines can also be found at www.ycnonline.com

Judging of work and award information

Work will initially be examined by the Zip Television team, led by Managing Partners Andrew Howells and Donna Barradale. They will prepare a shortlist of work for commendation and allocate their award pool and agency placements accordingly and at their discretion.

Commended submissions will go forward to the second round of judging to be hosted by London College of Fashion in July 2006. Further information on judging can be found at the start of this section and at www.ycnonline.com

Create a brand awareness campaign for BlackBerry

Background

BlackBerry® is a leading wireless connectivity solution, providing access to a wide range of applications on a variety of wireless devices around the world. It combines award-winning wireless devices, software and services to keep mobile professionals connected to the people, data and resources that drive their day.

BlackBerry keeps you 'in-the-loop' while you're on the go, with push-based technology that automatically delivers email and other data to your BlackBerry device. And with the integrated phone, SMS, browser and organizer applications, you can easily manage all your information and communications from a single, integrated device.

BlackBerry enables you to collaborate and communicate more effectively, and enhance your competitive advantage by responding quicker and making decisions faster. BlackBerry is the tool you need to stay connected and take care of business while you're on the go. It gives you the freedom to stay in touch with your work and home, with access to multiple existing corporate and/or personal email accounts from a single BlackBerry device.

We would strongly recommend you visit our website at www.blackberry.co.uk for more information about our services.

Beyond email

It should be noted that a BlackBerry solution goes further than just email and PIM functionality. Our open platform means that any Independent Software Vendor can write an application for the device. The applications can be standalone or can connect a BlackBerry device to a corporate network to provide access to a whole range of other data.

Our portfolio of products, services and embedded technologies include:
• BlackBerry® wireless platform
• Software and hardware licensing agreements
• BlackBerry device product line
• Software development tools
• Alliance programme
• ISV applications

Again, more information on this can be found at www.blackberry.co.uk

Why we are advertising

BlackBerry is about to enter an exciting period. The predictions from the analyst community, as well as our own intelligence, is that the market is on the verge of massive and fast growth. We also find ourselves with more competition. From software to device categories we see companies looking to exploit this growth. We are looking for excellent creative work, supported by sound strategic thinking, to meet these challenges head on.

Target audience

Business customers including; CEO's, Business managers and IT professionals in large corporate businesses, with a potentially significant mobile voice and data requirement.

Creative requirements

We are looking for fresh, new creative ideas that will raise the awareness of BlackBerry and drive interest in our products, services and solutions.
You are free to use any medium or combination of media that you choose to demonstrate your creative thinking. You should however bear in mind that your creative concepts will need to work across a number of marketing channels that would include press, poster and online. As well as your creative work we would also like you to submit an explanation of the strategy/ thinking behind your creative idea.

Mandatories

The BlackBerry logo should appear within your creative execution. This is available in the BlackBerry project pack at www.ycnonline.com

Deliverables

You should adhere to the main deliverables guidelines at the start of this section. These guidelines can also be found at www.ycnonline.com

Judging of work and award information

Work will initially be examined by a team led by Sarah West and Justin Hollis from BlackBerry. They will prepare a shortlist of work for commendation and allocate their award pool and agency placements accordingly and at their discretion.

Commended submissions will go forward to the second round of judging to be hosted by London College of Fashion in July 2006. Further information on judging can be found at the start of this section and at www.ycnonline.com

Produce a campaign or product that will engage and challenge the attitudes of people who dispose of chewing gum irresponsibly

Background
The irresponsible disposal of chewing gum is a high-profile issue for government, local councils and the public. Some councils spend up to £200,000 a year cleaning unsightly blobs from the streets. Chewing gum litter is often highlighted by the public as contributing to low environmental quality, and placed as a high-priority issue for their local councils to tackle. Even though dropping gum and other forms of litter is an offence that carries a £50 fine, it remains a significant problem and a priority for the current government.

To combat this, to raise awareness and to try and find sustainable solutions to the irresponsible disposal of gum, DEFRA work in partnership with chewing gum manufacturers and others through its Chewing Gum Action Group that was founded in the autumn of 2003.

Objective
The ultimate objective is to reduce the number of people that dispose of gum irresponsibly.

Target market
In order to define the target audience for the recent public awareness campaign, the Chewing Gum Action Group commissioned research designed to highlight the attitude of gum droppers. The findings revealed that many gum droppers fell into a group called 'excuses excuses'. People in this group knew it was wrong to drop gum, would do so

discretely and feel guilty afterwards. We believe that this group would be amenable to well targeted awareness campaigns.

Creative requirements

We are looking for a catchy, innovative visual awareness campaign or an alternative disposal solution. You are free to work in whichever medium, or combination of media, you see fit.

Mandatories

The campaign or disposal solution must not in anyway denigrate the chewing gum product.

Additional information

Further background on chewing gum as an environmental issue, the work of the Chewing Gum Action Group, the research on the attitudes of gum droppers and details of the public awareness pilot campaigns can be found at:

http://defraweb/environment /localenv/gum/index.htm

For details of the work and campaigns of EnCams visit : www.encams.org

Other useful websites : www.cleanersafergreener.gov.uk www.stubbi.com www.gumpouch.com

Deliverables

You should adhere to the main deliverables guidelines at the start of this section. These guidelines can also be found at www.ycnonline.com

Judging of work and award information

Work will initially be examined and assessed by members of the Chewing Gum Action Group led by Rory Wallace, Head of Local Environmental Quality, Defra. They will prepare a shortlist of work for commendation and allocate their award pool accordingly and at their discretion.

Commended submission will go forward to the second round of judging to be hosted by the London College of Fashion in July 2006. Further information on judging can be found at the start of this section and at www.ycnonline.com

For more than 30 years, Oakley has been obsessed with breaking the boundaries of innovation and technology. Create a campaign, using non-traditional means of communication, to amplify the Oakley brand among our 18-25 year old audience

Origin of the species
It started with a single idea. A mad scientist looked at a product and saw an opportunity. Jim Jannard created a world's first – a motocross handgrip with a unique orbicular design, engineered to fit a competitor's closed hand. The year was 1975. It was the beginning of Oakley Inc., a technology company that would soon be fueled by a raging distaste for mediocrity and a fierce devotion to innovation.

Today, Oakley is driven to seek out problems, create solutions, and wrap those solutions in art. The company's obsession with innovation has built a legacy of science, sculpture, and defiance of conventional thinking. Reinventing the concept of eyewear was only the first step. The passion that ignited the optical industry is now unleashed on high-performance footwear, consumer electronics, wristwatches, apparel and accessories.

A Global Brand
Infiltrating more than 70 countries around the world, Oakley has established itself as a global icon. Localised strategies of marketing and distribution maintain brand image and consistency among varying climates, cultures and continents by direct operations in Europe, Australia, New Zealand, South Africa, Mexico, Japan and Canada. In other parts of the world, the integrity of the brand is safeguarded by carefully selected distributors who present Oakley products to their markets with local expertise.

Action sports heritage
With the sponsorship of some of the worlds most revered athletes on the planet from surf, snow, skate, wakeboard, BMX, MX... Recent product developments in apparel, eyewear and consumer electronics has helped Oakley to transcend from being an action sports brand through to a lifestyle brand.

O Store London launched in Covent Garden in June 2005.

Our objective
Keep the brand messages simple and effective with a high visual/experiential impact.

Creative requirements
This brief is designed to maximise creativity and innovation and you should feel free to demonstrate your thinking in any non-traditional medium (or combination of media) that you see fit.

You may wish to consider:
• Regional or national campaigns
• Campaigns specific to a certain city
• Online communication

• Outdoor or ambient approaches
• Event-led ideas
• Other experiential approaches

Challenge and subvert the rules. Adopt any way of engaging the target market that you think will achieve maximum impact. You are free to create your own medium.

Target market
18-25 year olds of both sexes.

Mandatories
Where appropriate you should incorporate the Oakley logo into your work. this is available in the Oakley project pack at www.ycnonline.com

Deliverables
You should adhere to the main deliverables guidelines at the start of this section. These guidelines can also be found at www.ycnonline.com

Judging of work and award information
Work will initially be examined and assessed by a team led by Oakley Marketing Director, Alistair Franks and members of the media agency BJKE.

They will prepare a shortlist of work for commendation and allocate their award pool and agency placements accordingly and at their discretion.

Commended submission will go forward to the second round of judging to be hosted by the London College of Fashion in July 2006. Further information on judging can be found at the start of this section and at www.ycnonline.com

Explore creative solutions for how MB Games will attract and captivate a young game-playing market of the future (2010)

Background

MB Games encourage social interaction and the value of play – that's why Twister and Connect 4 are such perennial favourites.

We have a history of producing quality games that families trust and keep. Our brand portfolio also includes Operation, Buckaroo and Guess Who?.

All of our games are designed for kids, but there is a kid in all of us. We bring the whole family together, providing them with the opportunity to communicate with each other on the same level.

However, the family unit has changed and continues to change, affecting the families and children that we create games for. Nowadays children:
• Spend more time with adults other than their parents, e.g. nannies, aunts, grandparents etc.
• May have two family homes rather than one
• Have more holidays
• Spend more time on car and train journeys
• Are computer literate at a young age
• Have access to much more technology, eg. broadband internet access, mobile phones etc.
• Have more pocket money

When designing new games, we look at the key elements of traditional play, and constantly push its boundaries to respond to the way children and their families interact today.

It is important to bear in mind that 45% of children's games are bought by adults for children, so our games must appeal both to adults and children alike.

Objective
To address the social interaction of game playing in an exciting way. This can be through the design of a new game, a new approach to how games are played, or a new way of communicating game playing to a family in 2010.

We aim to expand our brand portfolio with a quality game that families in 2010 will trust and want to keep.

Key considerations
• Does the game bring the whole family together?
• Where can the game be played?

Target audience
Children aged 4 to 8 years, and their extended families.

Creative requirements
We want to encourage creativity and innovation across all creative disciplines.

We are looking for a product design, packaging design, point-of-sale material, advertising campaign, or even the complete package for:

• An adaptation of an existing MB game or games
• An entirely new MB game or games
• A new way of playing games

The concepts can be as broad or as focused as you deem suitable. They can be for an individual game or a group of games, maybe creating a new compendium for the family in 2010. You can work alone or in a group.

Mandatories
We want to see diverse, exciting, bold and innovative concepts that encourage social play as well as other values of play.

We don't want to see any computer/console games.

You should incorporate the MB logo somewhere into your work, as appropriate. This is available in the MB project pack at www.ycnonline.com

Additional information
Additional information regarding collaboration for the possible future development of MB Games submissions can be found in the MB Games project pack at www.ycnonline.com
More information about the company can be found at www.hasbro.co.uk

Deliverables
You should adhere to the main deliverables guidelines at the start of this section. These guidelines can also be found at www.ycnonline.com

Judging of work and award information
Work will initially be examined and assessed by a team headed by Alan Gong, head of design and development for Hasbro Europe, and Ben Rathbone, design director for Hasbro Europe. They will prepare a shortlist of work for commendation.

Commended submissions will go forward to the second round of judging to be hosted by London College of Fashion in July 2006. Further information on judging can be found at the start of this section and at www.ycnonline.com

How do you advertise to viewers when they don't watch the ads?

Background
The fundamentals of TV advertising are changing. It used to be that you could put a 30" ad in the middle of Coronation Street, and 18 million people would see it. Now, with Personal Video Recorders like Sky+, viewers record the programmes they want to watch and skip over the ads at the touch of a button. Ad avoidance is potentially a huge problem.

As young creatives setting out in advertising, you will be faced with writing and producing TV work that will have to work in a PVR world.

Objective
TV promotions / trailers are part of TV advertising. They are crucial in building channel brands as well as driving people to view new programmes.

We want ideas for TV promos (for programmes and channel services) that viewers won't skip through.

Targeting
Everyone who watches TV. Young, old, with kids, without. They love to watch the programmes but they're busy and impatient people.

Considerations

Don't think about the way we have promoted programmes and channel brands in the past. Think about this new PVR world where anything is possible. We can structure the ad breaks differently. We could have varying lengths of ad breaks. We could do something different in live programmes. We could do anything. We are looking for interesting and original ideas to grab people's attention.

Support Material

Look at current methods of programme promotion for reference. This includes:
• Programme trailers
• Channel idents / bumpers
• Channel menus
• Programme end-credit promotion
• In-programme continuity promotion

Examples of these kind of promotions can be seen in the Sky project pack at www.ycnonline.com.

Creative requirements

This brief has been kept deliberately very broad, and you are free to adopt any approach you wish in responding to it. How you go about demonstrating your creative thinking is up to you.

You might want to make your work specific to a certain programme, channel or other promotional aspect. The choice for this is up to you.

Deliverables

You should adhere to the main deliverables guidelines at the start of this section. These guidelines can also be found at www.ycnonline.com

Judging of work and award information

Work will initially be examined by a team led by Michael Hall, Sky Networks Head of Promotion Strategy. They will prepare a shortlist of work for commendation and allocate their award pool and agency placements accordingly and at their discretion.

Commended submissions will go forward to the second round of judging to be hosted by London College of Fashion in July 2006. Further information on judging can be found at the start of this section and at www.ycnonline.com

Create an ad campaign for a new Orange broadband offer

Background
Orange launched in 1994. Since launch Orange has always believed in the future and continues to do so. There is a fundamental optimism about everything we do, from how we behave to how we communicate.

The challenge
Orange is now extending its range of services to include landline (fixed line) services, specifically broadband. The challenge is to create an ad campaign for a £17.99 a month broadband offer. The offer should clearly be from Orange and reflect everything we stand for. Things like optimism and a human tone of voice are a must!

Creative formats
An ad campaign in any format.

Considerations
Considering where you advertise is just as important as what you advertise. Advertising space is forever finding new territory. Sometimes this new territory dictates how you advertise. A well-improvised advertising location or solution can often give a company a much-needed edge over its competitors, so don't just consider how you advertise, but also where.

It's entirely down to you how you demonstrate your creative thinking.

Deliverables
You should adhere to the main deliverables guidelines at the start of this section. These guidelines can also be found at www.ycnonline.com

Judging of work and award information
Work will initially be examined by a team led by Ben Spencer from Orange. They will prepare a shortlist of work for commendation and allocate their award pool and agency placements accordingly and at their discretion.

Commended submissions will go forward to the second round of judging to be hosted by London College of Fashion in July 2006. Further information on judging can be found at the start of this section and at www.ycnonline.com

Create a magazine for children aged 6-11, to be read during the summer holidays

Background
John Brown Junior is a division of John Brown Citrus Publishing, and has a reputation for creating original, imaginative content for children. Previous publications have been created for brands such as Sky, the British Heart Foundation and Disney.

Creative objective
To conceive of an engaging magazine for kids aged 6-11, filled with fun ideas and games to keep them entertained throughout the long summer holiday.

Issues to consider:
• it has to be attractive for boys and girls
• it should be fun to read and to look at
• the market is filled with identikit comics and magazines; try to think imaginatively, without being too obtuse for the intended market
• think from the perspective of children - history should be horrible, houses ought to be haunted, zoos should be filled with creatures that are deadly, freaky or funny...
• kids prefer not to have to call in a parent to help, so keep any tasks simple

Creative requirements
• Maximum of 500 words explaining the concept for your magazine, and the thinking behind it
• Magazine name
• Logo design
• Front cover design(s)
• Example spreads demonstrating the overall design

Deliverables
You should adhere to the main deliverable guidelines at the start of this section. These guidelines can also be found at www.ycnonline.com

Judging of work and award information
Work will initially be examined and assessed by a team at John Brown Citrus Publishing, headed by Jeremy Leslie, Chris Parker and Sara Lynn. They will prepare a shortlist of work for commendation and allocate their award pool and agency placements accordingly and at their discretion.

Commended submissions will go forward to the second round of judging to be hosted by London College of Fashion in July 2006. Further information on judging can be found at the start of this section and at www.ycnonline.com

John
Brown
Citrus
Publishing

Develop a campaign that communicates the Nobby's brand essence of 'straightforward satisfaction' to blokes aged 18 to 35.

Background.

"Nibble Nobby's, Not Noddy's!..." Nobby's has been one of the biggest and most successful FMCG brand launches of 2005. A hugely successful media campaign fronted by legendary 70s rocker Noddy Holder has made Nobby's famous, and already begun to build a loyal consumer base. However, Nobby's is still a very young brand, and the next step is to begin to establish an identity for Nobby's beyond the launch campaign that centres on the essence of 'straightforward satisfaction' that will entrench the brand in the hearts of the British male.

Nobby's brand essence is 'Straightforward Satisfaction' – sometimes ordinary snacks aren't enough to really satisfy, you just want more taste and flavour. Step forward Nobby's: great tasting snacks that fill you up.

Nobby's is a brand that understands what blokes want. If Nobby was in your local pub, he would be that easy-going bloke at the bar, who always tells it like it is and, of course, is always first to get the beers in! Nobby's is all about humour (more Peter Kay than Johnny Vegas), generosity and no bullshit.

Nobby's is a brand platform that currently stretches across crisps and nuts, but with a plan to develop many other formats that stretch into more filling real food snacks.

Objective
To communicate the essence of straightforward satisfaction, and make Nobby's the snack of choice for 18-35 males.

The Creative challenge
We are looking for creative ideas that will connect with the target audience, and communicate to them the essence of the Nobby's brand.

Apart from TV and radio, it's entirely down to you which media you choose to work in. Think creatively about the best way to reach the target market at the times (and in the places) that they'll be most receptive to the message.

You may wish to demonstrate your creative across several different media or you may wish to focus on just one.

You should consider that competition for the attention of 18-35 year old blokes is fierce, and the creative solution will need to effectively cut through the array of other advertising aimed at this group.

Mandatories
Where appropriate you should incorporate the Nobby's logo into your work. This can be found in the Nobby's project pack at www.ycnonline.com

Additional information
You can find information about what Nobby's is and what it isn't in the Nobby's project pack at www.ycnonline.com

Deliverables
You should adhere to the main deliverables guidelines at the start of this section. These guidelines can also be found at www.ycnonline.com

Judging of work and award information
Work will initially be examined by a team led by Charles Leslie from Nobby's. They will prepare a shortlist of work for commendation and allocate their award pool and agency placements accordingly and at their discretion.

Commended submissions will go forward to the second round of judging to be hosted by London College of Fashion in July 2006. Further information on judging can be found at the start of this section and at www.ycnonline.com

Dorling Kindersley

Create a new preschool book format and graphic design style for a global market

Background

Dorling Kindersley (DK) is a leading brand in book publishing for preschool children. Research shows that the preschool years are the foundation of all future learning. Parents can share books with babies and toddlers right from birth – reading, talking, singing, pointing. A fun and warm experience encourages children to want to read books, and continue reading, for life.

We write and design our preschool books inhouse in our UK offices. We publish them under our own brand in the US, Australia, Canada and South Africa, and we sell our books to foreign-language publishers in almost every other territory across the world.

In the 1980s, we were the first publishers to use photography as illustration. We developed a distinct style, using cut-out images on a white background, precisely labelled. We are now facing stiff competition from publishers reproducing the same look.

Another important trend in the preschool books market is the use of novelty formats. Flaps, pop-ups, sound chips, touch and feel textures – our competitors have been producing books with add-ons that really grab consumers' attention.

Objective

To create book formats that are innovative both in their physicality and in their graphic design, to retain our market share.

Our consumer

We know that our books are mostly bought by Mums who:
• are first-time Mums
• are having babies later in life
• are having fewer children altogether
• have often had a career
• are as sophisticated in their book buying as clothes buying
• like to feel that a book benefits their child's development
• like to enjoy the books themselves
• like books to accessorize their homes

Creative requirements

Think about:

What size and shape is the book, does it fit on bookstore shelves?

What kind of paper or other materials is it made from? – babies chew books! There are also safety issues to consider – certain substances and fabrics that could be toxic or parts that could become choking hazards if pulled off.

What fun, strong add-ons would you use?

How can you use the paper itself to add play value – folds, cut-through, popups etc?

What kind of illustration appeals to children and their parents – if you use photography, how is this different from what we already do?

You don't need many words – babies love rhythm, repetition and rhyme.

Our best-selling subjects are: farm, baby animals, first words, first numbers, nursery rhymes – use these, or your own.
You can deliver either a whole book, or a front cover and some sample pages.

Mandatories

Use the DK logo on the front cover. This can be found in the DK project pack at www.ycnonline.com

Deliverables

You should adhere to the main deliverables guidelines at the start of this section. These guidelines can also be found at www.ycnonline.com

Judging of work and award information

Work will initially be examined by a team led by Liz Statham from DK. They will prepare a shortlist of work for commendation and allocate their award pool and agency placements accordingly and at their discretion.

Commended submissions will go forward to the second round of judging to be hosted by London College of Fashion in July 2006. Further information on judging can be found at the start of this section and at www.ycnonline.com

Come up with a name for SKY's potential new portable media player and devise a campaign to launch it

Background

Sky+ is a Sky box and digital video recorder all in one.

It allows you to record TV without any hassle. Programmes are stored on a hard drive in the Sky+ box, so no need for tapes. Playback is digital with all the regular features of pause, fast forward, rewind, slow motion. Sky+ also allows you to pause and rewind live TV – giving you so much more control. It really changes the way you watch TV.

The Sky+ service is great, but imagine a portable media player associated with the Sky+ service which allowed you to take your stored programmes with you.

This device would allow you to download content from the Sky+ box to the portable device to watch anywhere you choose. The device would be handheld, portable with easy-to-use keys and a screen.

Objectives

1) Come up with a name for the product that fits with the Sky+ and Sky brand.

2) Devise a launch campaign that positions Sky's portable media player as an easy to use, accessible and fun product that allows you to view TV on the move.

3) The campaign needs to work across all media.

Who are we talking to?
Parents of children – bustling families with kids in the 5-12yrs range looking for solutions to viewing conflicts or something to keep the kids busy on car journeys.

Urban Commuters – busy professionals who don't want to miss their favourite TV, and can combine the convenience of Sky+ recording when they are out with a portable device that can help them utilize that spare 30mins on the train to catch up with their favourite soap or US drama.

Proposition
• Watch your favourite TV on the move
• Why should they believe us?
• Sky+ allows you to easily record your favourite TV and this device is portable and handheld which allows you to watch your favourite shows on the move.

Tone of voice
Sky values are tuned in, irrepressible, inviting and fun

Media
The choice of media you choose to demonstrate your launch campaign is entirely down to you but the creative idea will need to work across a range of channels including TV, outdoor, direct mail, internet and press advertising.

Additional Information
www.sky.com

Sky+ brand guidelines are available in the Sky+ project pack at www.ycnonline.com

For an idea of the range of currently available portable media devices look at Sony PSP, Archos.com, Microsoft portable media players, Creative Zen Vision etc.

Deliverables
You should adhere to the main deliverables guidelines at the start of this section. These guidelines can also be found at www.ycnonline.com

Judging of work and award information
Work will initially be examined by a team led by Paul Wilson from Sky. They will prepare a shortlist of work for commendation and allocate their award pool and agency placements accordingly and at their discretion.

Commended submissions will go forward to the second round of judging to be hosted by London College of Fashion in July 2006. Further information on judging can be found at the start of this section and at www.ycnonline.com

Disrupt young males drinking routine and convince them to try J&B -6°c

Background

What is J&B -6°c?

J&B -6°c is a new blended Scotch Whisky from Justerini and Brooks (J&B). The J&B brand has a heritage that dates back to 1749, and J&B RARE blended Scotch Whisky was first produced in Scotland in 1910. Now, Justerini & Brooks has used its expertise, and its wide range of maturing grain and malt Whiskies, to blend J&B -6°c, a smooth and subtle-tasting Scotch Whisky for a new generation of Whisky drinkers.

The specially selected grains and unusually high malt content that goes into the blend create the subtle flavour of J&B -6°c, and give it a naturally light colour.

The unique flavour of J&B -6°c blended Scotch Whisky makes it great for mixing with tonic, lemonade, cranberry, and ginger ale, but it is equally good neat or over ice.

How is J&B -6°c different from other Whiskies?

While some traditional Whiskies can be smoky, peaty and challenging, J&B -6°c blended Scotch Whisky has been blended for a lighter, more subtle style with fresh notes which remind us of apple and pear.

Why is it called J&B -6°c?

The name -6°c is inspired by the chill filtration process used when making this great Whisky. When we spoke to people about the name. they found it contemporary and appealing, so we stuck with it

What gives it its unique smooth and subtle taste?

Our Master Blenders carefully selected malts and grain Whiskies from our stocks with the freshest green notes, which remind us of apples and pears. In addition, J&B -6°c blended Scotch Whisky contains an unusually high malt content relative to other blends.

These malt and grain Whiskies are then carefully blended to create a contemporary style of Whisky (and not a certain age) that wows Whisky and non-Whisky drinkers alike. We therefore used a mix of young and old Whiskies to achieve this.

What gives J&B -6°c its distinctive colour?

Whisky colour, aroma and taste are derived from the raw materials used. The malt and grain Whiskies, selected by our Master Blenders for their unique taste, are naturally light in colour.

What does J&B -6°c taste of?

Aroma: Light and fresh with notes of cut grass, green banana, almond and cereal.
Taste: Vanilla sweetness and hazelnut are balanced with green apple and fresh fruits to give a light, refreshing flavour.
Finish: A short, fresh, malty finish with just a hint of spice.

J&B -6°c is reinventing Whisky and making it more relevant to a younger audience. It was launched in specially selected bars in April 2005.

Brand proposition

A surprisingly clean and fresh taste delivered through a chill filtered blend of J&B -6°c.

Why should people believe this?
• Functional: Unexpected whisky, whisky with clarity, drinkable, mixable, smooth.
• Emotional: Shows that I am progressing intelligently.

Primary communication
J&B -6°c Whisky has been reinvented. It's here to make you challenge your perceptions and try whisky: different.

Brand personality
Confident, Surprising, Intelligent, Masculine and Stylish.

Tone of voice
Challenging but not revolutionary. Credible and authentic.

Current creative platform
The platform for communicating the unique proposition offered by J&B -6°c blended Scotch Whisky has been "See Through Convention", which prompts consumers to put aside their perceptions of Scotch as a conventional category, and to consider J&B -6°c.

This can be used as a strapline or utilized in your approach somehow, but this is not mandatory.

Who are we talking to?
Specifically it will be of high appeal to discerning 25-35 year old males, who generally perceive the Scotch Whisky category as unappealing, as it is surrounded by confusing terminology, harsh taste perceptions, and traditional imagery that does not fit with today's trends.

A more detailed description of our target consumer can be found in this brief's project pack at www.ycnonline.com

What our target consumers think and/or do now
"I'm not really a scotch drinker – it tastes too harsh and it's more of an old-man's drink".
"I drink lager mainly, and Jack Daniels and vodka when it comes to spirits."
"I have never really heard of J&B."

What we want them to think and / or do as a result of this activity
There's a new whisky out called J&B -6°c.
It's completely different from other whiskies – much smoother, more modern and versatile.
I will really like the taste.
I might try it next time I'm out.

Media
You can approach this brief in any fashion that you choose and can demonstrate your thinking in whichever medium, or combination of media, you see fit.

Mandatories
There can be no communication of the whisky using the words: clear, clarity, white, whisky (SWA regulations).

The submission must meet the letter and spirit of the Diageo Marketing Code. This can be found in the project pack at www.ycnonline.com

The brand name must be used as J&B -6°c and not split to -6°c.

Where appropriate, you should incorporate the J&B-6°c logo into your work. This can be found in the project pack at www.ycnonline.com

Responsible Drinking
Information relating to the sensitivities surrounding the advertising of alcohol can be found in the project pack at www.ycnonline.com

Deliverables
You should adhere to the main deliverables guidelines at the start of this section. These guidelines can also be found at www.ycnonline.com

Judging of work and award information
Work will initially be examined by a team led by Penny Welch from Diageo. They will prepare a shortlist of work for commendation and allocate their award pool and agency placements accordingly and at their discretion.

Commended submissions will go forward to the second round of judging to be hosted by London College of Fashion in July 2006. Further information on judging can be found at the start of this section and at www.ycnonline.com

The AOL brief can be found in full at the ycn website

The AOL brief was not complete at the time of publication but can be found in full, along with all of this year's briefs, at www.ycnonline.com

Deliverables
You should adhere to the main deliverables guidelines at the start of this section. These guidelines can also be found at www.ycnonline.com

Judging of work and award information
Work will initially be examined by a team led by David Pagliari and Chris Davis from AOL. They will prepare a shortlist of work for commendation and allocate their award pool and agency placements accordingly and at their discretion.

Commended submissions will go forward to the second round of judging to be hosted by London College of Fashion in July 2006. Further information on judging can be found at the start of this section and at www.ycnonline.com

Devise a creative
concept that will make
8-11 year olds want to
buy Bootleg shoes
from Clarks

Background
Bootleg is a brand that produces
footwear for 8-11 year old boys
and girls. It is a sub brand of
Clarks. Bootleg was initially
launched as a school footwear
brand. Sports shoes were
introduced to the range in 2002.

The Bootleg brand was launched
in 1995 as a way of Clarks
retaining young customers who
are beginning to reject Clarks for
brands they feel are more
credible. They no longer find it
acceptable to wear products that
are branded Clarks (it's what
their little brothers are wearing),
but their mothers are keen to
keep them in well-fitted, well-
made footwear for as long as
possible. Bootleg enjoys all the
same core values as the Clarks
brand (which is why mum is so
keen to keep her child in Bootleg
product). Bootleg shoes are
always properly fitted by trained
experts, which is unique for a
shoe brand for 8-11 year olds; the
product is available in whole and
half sizes, and a choice of widths
to find the perfect fit. All product
has three month's growing room
built in, a real plus point for
mum. All this is great for mum
but not something that kids seem
to care about.

The Bootleg product is positioned
in the kids' department of a
Clarks store. It is at the furthest
point from the youngest
shoppers, and is displayed on a
silver sports shop style wall.
Product is displayed side facing
on single shelves.

Twice yearly, we have a dedicated Bootleg window that will feature boys' and girls' Bootleg product.

The instore presentation of the Bootleg brand has changed dramatically over the past ten years, from traditional lifestyle, too more recently an illustrative approach. A single Bootleg handwriting has never been established.

Distinctive POS is particularly important for Bootleg, as it helps to distinguish Bootleg from other brands that it may be sitting alongside, ie. Clarks and CICA (Clarks' own sports brand) in Clarks shops, and brands such as Kickers, Nike and pods in independents.

Target audience
Boys and girls aged 8-11 with some spill over into 7 and 12 year olds)

It is not necessary for the graphics to be relevant to the parents of the target audience.

The 8-11 year old target audience for Bootleg is a difficult one, as they are more sophisticated than their younger Clarks buying brothers and sisters but not yet teenagers. This group of youngsters is sometimes referred to as 'tweens'. There are differing levels of maturity between boys and girls of this age – this manifests itself in their hobbies, interests, aspirations, relationship with fashion and their consumer behaviour. There is a temptation to overestimate the maturity and sophistication of this audience. The mums of our Bootleg customers have an inherent understanding of the importance of fitted shoes. They probably have to be quite persuasive to get their child to still visit a Clarks store.

Creative requirements
Your creative concept will need to work across a range of channels. These will include press advertising, our website and importantly, the Clarks store windows.

You are free though to bring your idea to life in as many different media as you please. However, if you would prefer to focus on just one channel, then this should be how your creative concept would work in the store window display.

Creative considerations
Examples of past window displays along with dimensions and other considerations can be found in the Clarks project pack at www.ycnonline.com

Your creative concept should appeal to boys and girls. Although any communication needs to be aimed at kids, you will need to bear in mind that mum is the one paying for the shoes.

Additional guidelines pertinent to the Bootleg brand can be found as a PDF in the Clarks project pack at www.ycnonline.com

Tone and Character
• Cool (to the eyes of a ten year old)
• Rebellious (but still ok with mum)
• Confident and credible
• Not at all like Clarks!

Mandatories
The Bootleg logo, which can be found in the Clarks project pack at www.ycnonline.com

Deliverables
You should adhere to the main deliverables guidelines at the start of this section. These guidelines can also be found at www.ycnonline.com

Judging of work and award information
Work will initially be examined by a team led by Ted Clark, Ian Hart and Alice Mounter from Clarks. They will prepare a shortlist of work for commendation and allocate their award pool and agency placements accordingly and at their discretion.

Commended submissions will go forward to the second round of judging to be hosted by London College of Fashion in July 2006. Further information on judging can be found at the start of this section and at www.ycnonline.com

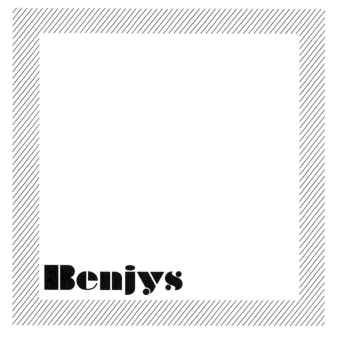

Challenge existing perceptions of Benjys and get new customers in store

Background

In the last two years the perception of Benjys has changed from being 'cheap and cheerful' to being great value for money. Benjys now firmly 'owns' this positioning within the sandwich sector.

As a brand however, Benjys currently fails to appeal to a large number of the working population of London who still have a misconception of the food quality, packaging and presentation, customer service, store environment and range (which includes hot food as well as sandwiches).

In a strong London market this may not be an issue for the brand as there is sufficient business within its core market. However, maintaining this core market along with the emergence of a large number of small-format supermarkets competing in the same value and convenience space means Benjys needs to broaden its appeal to new users while preventing existing users from moving elsewhere.

Benjys most significant point of difference is its hot food counter which serves made-to-order hot food for both breakfast and lunch. This is one area that is currently not strongly promoted and most people walking past our shops are not aware that we have a hot food counter.

We know that the primary motivator of our customers is convenience followed by quality followed by choice. Further consumer research indicates that there is a divergence in the marketplace whereby shoppers opt for two very different types of product: 1) healthy, or 2) indulgent. More specifically, customer behaviour indicates there are those that choose healthily most of the time, and there are those that decide that, if they are going to have something, they are going to buy something that is an indulgent treat (sweet/fatty etc).

Potential new users are turned off by a perception of cheap or variable quality. They are also more aware of 'store environments' both in terms of look, presentation and staff. They would be amazed to think of Benjys as Manufacturer, Retailer and Marketeer of the Year.

They know they overpay at Pret and EAT but enjoy the combinations of food ingredients, and suffer no associated stigma of where they go for lunch. We now need to appeal to these potential new customers by tweaking our message range (especially with an emphasis on hot food) and instore format without alienating existing users.

Objectives

To change non-users' perceptions about Benjys' quality and food credentials and get 1 million new customers into our stores over the next 12 months.

To astound existing users so that, when they visit Benjys, they are amazed that it has a hot food range, and is the same store/brand as before, due to the leading-edge, high-quality look and feel of the store.

Who are we advertising to?

People working or studying in London at least 3 times a week, mainly between 6am and 5pm. Primarily they will be non-Benjys users who are traditional Pret and EAT customers. It is recognised that we 'own' the value positioning, and that although it is an important driver, quality and convenience are greater motivators for non-users. Hence we are using food credentials of both cold and hot food ranges to sell the product, and leaving the value aspect to speak for itself.

In terms of positioning, this could mean maintaining the "leading sandwich retailer" position, while introducing a Benjys "Deli and Grill"-type concept to support our hot food range.

Insights

Quality is the overriding driver for new users of Benjys (those of under two years), compared to customers of over two years who shop with us for value.

Food provenance is important to underscore the quality, together with a reasonable price (not too cheap).

Convenience is the biggest factor in purchasing habits, and increasing density of outlets means it is harder to retain customers.

Risk of making a bad decision, and therefore not having any lunch, because you haven't the time to go out again. Consistency is key to a quality image.

Trust within the 'food scare' environment in the quality of ingredients and the handling of the products in store. Service, which has to be fast and efficient.

Staff must have the ability to respond to customer issues appropriately, ie. an English-speaking company with a positive service mentality.

Advertising proposition

Benjys is the indisputable value champion. Both users and non-users alike would recognise this position – this must remain a 'given'. Quality must now become the primary message of communication; we are the smart man's choice, not the poor man's choice. Range must be emphasised – we are a lunchtime retailer but our USP is our hot food range.

Tone/personality

Down to earth, friendly and trustworthy with a quirky and irreverent approach. Food credentials are very important, and making the food the hero of the business is key. Value is so obvious, it's a given that the customer knows we are and remain the value champion. More cool and contemporary than before, we must appeal to a broader church of users who are conscious of what their lunch says about them.

Desired response

Hot food range clearly communicated and understood.

Brand perception of quality to be significantly increased, and appeal to non-users maximised.

Use of media

You are free to respond to the brief and demonstrate your creative thinking in whichever medium or combination of media you see fit, but do bare in mind that our communication budgets are small so we are looking for low-cost, high-impact thinking!

Feel free to explore conventional or new communication tactics. You may wish to consider how we can be creative in store. Creativity on the street or in any other channel that will connect with our target audience, and fulfil our ambitions, will also be of interest.

Mandatories

Where appropriate, you should incorporate the Benjys logo into your work. This is available in the Benjys project pack at the ycn website.

Deliverables

You should adhere to the main deliverables guidelines at the start of this section. These guidelines can also be found at www.ycnonline.com

Judging of work and award information

Work will initially be examined by a team led by Emma Rickwood from Benjys. They will prepare a shortlist of work for commendation and allocate their award pool and agency placements accordingly and at their discretion.

Commended submissions will go forward to the second round of judging to be hosted by London College of Fashion in July 2006. Further information on judging can be found at the start of this section and at www.ycnonline.com

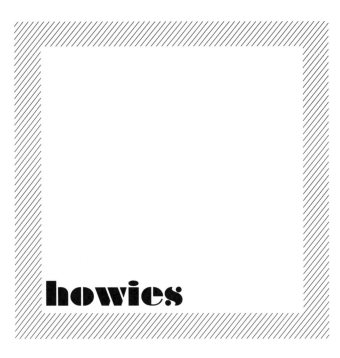

Create an illustration based on the theme of Hope to appear on a howies t-shirt

Background

howies is a small, active clothing company based in Cardigan Bay, on the west coast of Wales. It is Cardigan Bay's 3rd biggest clothing company.

It makes high-quality clothing for the sports it loves; mountain biking, skateboarding, snowboarding and the outdoors.

It has a certain way of doing things. It believes in quality and in making products that last longer, which is better for the environment in the long run. It also believes in making products in a low-impact way. (For example, all its t-shirts, sweatshirts, cords etc are made from organic cotton.)

Its mission is to make people think about stuff, and it uses the t-shirts as a vehicle to do this. They act as a running social commentary.

It tries to entertain people into thinking rather than ranting at people.

Its t-shirts, which sell really well, are designed by top illustrators, artists, typographers and graphic designers, as well as being designed in-house.

The howies tone of voice
Not too serious, not too preachy.
Our T-shirts should entertain,
inspire, question but not rant.
They should make us laugh and
make us think. They can be
clever, silly, ironic, or whatever.

You can illustrate words, pictures
or anything else for that matter
as long as the work feels true to
howies. The best ideas just
connect with how people think or
where they are in their lives right
now.

The brief is only a starting point.
Every year we send out a brief,
and every year the best t-shirts
are the ones that strayed a wee
bit from it. Like any brief, this is
only a guide – to help you focus
but not to hinder. At the very
least, you can have a piece of
paper as a starting point. The aim
is to illustrate something that
says something. To use your
illustration to make a point. But
also to remember at the end of
the day that you want to wear it
because it looks good.

Target audience
Skateboarders, mountain bikers,
snowboarders and all those who
think about stuff.

Mandatory
Have fun. Do what you love.
Always make tea in a pot.

You can submit as many or as few
ideas as you like.

More info
www.howies.co.uk
or see the new catalogue

Deliverables
You should adhere to the main
deliverables guidelines at the
start of this section. These
guidelines can also be found at
www.ycnonline.com

**Judging of work and award
information**
Work will initially be examined
by a team led by David Hieatt
from howies. They will prepare a
shortlist of work for
commendation and decide which
t-Shirts are produced as part of a
limited-edition howies range.

Commended submissions will go
forward to the second round of
judging to be hosted by London
College of Fashion in July 2006.
Further information on judging
can be found at the start of this
section and at
www.ycnonline.com

howies®

The Thinkbox Award for outstanding creativity in television.

As a brand new addition to this year's awards, Thinkbox is partnering with ycn to celebrate submissions that make the very best creative and innovative use of TV.

What is Thinkbox?

Thinkbox is the new television marketing body for all the UK commercial channels – Channel 4, Five, GMTV, ids, ITV, Sky, Turner and Viacom.

For the first time ever, all the channels have joined forces to help customers get more out of TV.

Creative use of television

Great creative ideas are at the heart of the very best TV marketing, and today's TV has more opportunities than ever to bring your ideas to life. The advent of interactive television, branded content, 'blipverts', stings and break bumpers are just some of the innovations that have seen TV shift into a new era of innovative and engaging advertising.

We recognise that encouraging the creative talent of the future will ensure that TV continues to be one of the most exciting and dynamic industries to be a part of. This is why we're partnering with ycn for this year's awards.

What we will be looking for

The Thinkbox panel will be examining all of the best work submitted as part of this year's awards, and will identify those to have made the most fresh and inspiring use of TV in their entries. Full details of how this judging will work, the panel, and a host of other content and creative examples can be found in the dedicated Thinkbox section of the ycn website.

What the Thinkbox award will offer

We want to help you launch your career and as such will be awarding Gold, Silver and Bronze awards for the most innovative use of TV.

The winners will be offered the opportunity to enter into a unique 12-month creative mentoring programme to kick start their careers and give them an up-close and hands-on experience of TV advertising. There will also be an additional award for the overall Gold winner, full details of which can be found, alongside extensive details of how this programme will work, at the ycn website.

We're here to help

If you need to learn more about how today's TV can works for your submission, we're here to help. We can put you in touch with experts, and provide a plethora of information to help you explore the creative opportunities TV can offer for your challenge.

You can visit Thinkbox at www.thinkbox.tv, or email us at info@thinkbox.tv

doodle
scribble
draw
stick